PLANNING PRIMARY
SCIENCE

PLANNING PRIMARY
SCIENCE

REVISED NATIONAL CURRICULUM EDITION

**Key Stages
1&2**

Revised by
Roy Richardson
Education Adviser

Original material by
Roy Richardson
Phillip Coote
Alan Wood

JOHN MURRAY

Other titles in the **Key Strategies** series:

English Speaking and Listening by Gordon Lamont

From Talking to Handwriting by Daphne M. Tasker

Helping with Handwriting by Rosemary Sassoon

Music: A Practical Guide for Teachers by Alan Biddle and Lynn Dolby

Physical Education: A Practical Guide by Elizabeth Robertson

Planning Primary Design and Technology by Roy Richardson

Planning Primary Geography by Maureen Weldon and Roy Richardson

Planning Primary History by Tim Lomas, Christine Burke, Dave Cordingley, Karen McKenzie and Lesley Tyreman

Primary Science: A Complete Reference Guide by Michael Evans

Cover photograph: Martin Dohrn/Science Photo Library

Material from the National Curriculum
is Crown copyright and is reproduced
by permission of the Controller of HMSO.

© Roy Richardson 1993, 1996
© Phillip Coote, Alan Wood 1993

First published in 1993
by John Murray (Publishers) Ltd
50 Albemarle Street
London W 1X 4BD

Second edition 1996

Reprinted 1997

Layouts by Mick McCarthy
Line drawings by Tom Cross

Typeset in 10½/12 Rockwell by Wearset, Boldon, Tyne and Wear
Printed in Great Britain by St Edmundsbury Press, Bury St Edmunds

A CIP catalogue record for this book is available from the British Library.

ISBN 0-7195-7244-4

Contents

CONTENTS

Introduction

PLANNING FOR SCIENCE THROUGH KEY STAGES 1 AND 2

This support material is aimed to help primary schools review, or make a fresh start in implementing, the statutory Orders for science. It sets out clearly the process which all schools will need to complete in order to write their Science Policy and Scheme of Work, both of which are legal responsibilities for all headteachers and governing bodies.

It is a legal requirement for all primary schools to give each child access to the Programmes of Study for science. Primary teachers need knowledge, confidence and guidance to give children this entitlement and to ensure quality of learning. We hope that the material in this book will assist teachers to plan and deliver this entitlement.

Schools have now received details of the new revised Orders for all the core and foundation subjects, each one demanding time and effort to implement. Many schools are therefore now undertaking a review of each curriculum area and perhaps their original plans and styles of delivery.

It can be a lengthy task to map out the entitlement and headteachers, as curriculum managers, need to ensure that no aspect of the Orders is neglected or omitted. Staff need the support of a long-term plan, or Programme for Science, which will save them considerable time in the early stages, and will provide a basis for planning scientific investigations and activities for all children.

To meet this need chapter 5 shows clearly how teachers can draw up a Programme for Science in which they can map out the entire content of science throughout Key Stages 1 and 2, irrespective of the size of the school or how children's age groups are arranged within it.

Time is a commodity which primary schools find is in short supply at present. An example Science Policy (pages 10–12) and Programme for Science (page 25) have been included which schools may choose to adopt, or adapt, to suit their own situation and ethos.

The example Science Policy and Programme for Science have been used to create a Scheme of Work for science (pages 31–162) which could again be used by schools of any size and any combination of mixed-age classes.

Chapter 6 gives examples of scientific activities and investigations that ensure coverage of the statutory Orders for science. The examples are set down in units of work matched to the Programme for Science so that teachers can see clearly what has to be covered and how. The activities and investigations are designed to provide a minimum that schools will need to achieve in order to deliver their statutory requirements.

Curriculum development is progressive and schools will need to set down a realistic timetable from its inception. Headteachers will need to ensure that science planning is given priority during this period.

We hope that this book will assist primary school teachers to draw up or review their plans for science so that ultimately children will benefit from an improved quality of teaching.

Roy Richardson, Phillip Coote and Alan Wood

Before making a start . . .

The role of headteachers in any curriculum development is crucial and without their total commitment, support and guidance it is pointless making a start. Headteachers need to give their time to define the timescale for planning and reviewing and ensure that priority will be given to achieving the required aims.

Drawing up a Science Policy, or dividing the science statutory Orders into units to be taught by individual teachers, is relatively easy and takes little time. The pressure on primary schools to implement all areas of the National Curriculum as quickly as possible is great and this approach to implementing science has been common but leads to only short-term gains. Headteachers and staff need to treat the process of implementing the science Orders as a whole, and lay down what is expected of each individual and the timescale involved in order to ensure not only coverage but quality teaching experiences for children.

Staff will need to set or be set clear and understandable criteria by which the success of each stage of the teaching and assessment processes can be measured. It is pointless to launch a new science programme unless everyone involved has a clear idea of what is expected from them as individuals, and as part of a teaching team.

Quality in any sphere takes time to achieve and to obtain quality you require a concise image of your goals. The teaching of science is no exception.

1 WHAT IS GOOD SCIENCE TEACHING?

Setting standards

All schools should take an overall approach to the planning and reviewing of any curriculum area. At the outset of drawing up a Science Policy, all the teachers involved should have:

1. An agreed view of what they consider to be good science teaching. This will help staff to see exactly what they and the school are aiming to achieve.
2. A clear understanding of what the statutory Orders for science state and a thorough knowledge of exactly the science for which they have to ensure coverage.

This background will help staff when they draw up their Programme for Science and decide which aspect of science should be taught when, and whose responsibility it is to teach it.

WHAT IS GOOD SCIENCE?

Science in the primary school is concerned with children finding out about the world in which they live. It involves children developing knowledge and understanding of themselves and the world around them.

Science work in school helps children to develop their **knowledge and understanding** of scientific concepts enabling them to learn and use the **skills** associated with scientific methods of investigation. It fosters **attitudes** that promote scientific ways of thinking and working, such as curiosity, co-operation and sensitivity to living organisms. All these elements of learning are set out within the four Sections of the Programme of Study which make up the statutory Orders for science.

Knowledge Children need to be given opportunities to experience all areas of scientific knowledge which can be of use to them in their lives and in new situations. These areas of study are defined within Sc2, 3 and 4.

Skills 'All children should have the opportunity to develop the skills of imaginative but disciplined enquiry' (National Curriculum Science Working Group, *Interim Report*, 1988). The skills of working as a scientist involve observation, hypothesis, design, investigation and the ability to draw conclusions and communicate effectively. All these aspects need to be developed in children, and are defined within Sc1 of the science curriculum.

Attitudes Attitudes such as curiosity, perseverance and co-operation are developed through scientific activities.

2 WHAT ARE THE STATUTORY REQUIREMENTS?

Statutory requirements for schools when planning for science

To establish what the statutory Orders for science are asking teachers to plan, staff need to have a clear understanding of each aspect of the Orders. The Orders are made up of the following sections:
1. Common Requirements
2. Introductory Section
3. Sections of the Programme of Study
4. Level Descriptions.

COMMON REQUIREMENTS

The Common Requirements give guidance on ways of providing access for the great majority of children, the use of language, information technology, referencing with examples printed in italics.

When planning it is important to take note of the following aspects of the Common Requirements:
- that every effort should be made to provide access to the Orders for all children irrespective of any special needs. To assist teachers in meeting this requirement they can select material from earlier or later Key Stages if more appropriate;
- that due attention should be given to children's use of both oral and written language within science lessons;
- that pupils should, where appropriate, be given opportunities to develop and apply their information technology capability within science activities;
- that the referencing system used in the Orders does not indicate a teaching sequence or hierarchy of knowledge, understanding and skills;
- that the examples in italics are non-statutory.

INTRODUCTORY SECTION

This Section contains a set of general requirements for each Key Stage. Many important aspects are set down within the Introductory Section. It is important that teachers are fully aware of the requirements and include them in their planning. The requirements are set down under five headings and clearly state that children should be given opportunities to study the following:

1. Systematic enquiry
- ask questions;
- ask questions related to their work (Key Stage 2);
- acquire scientific knowledge, understanding and skills through focused exploration and investigations;
- use first hand experience and simple secondary sources to obtain information;
- use IT to collect, store, retrieve and present information.

2. Science in everyday life
- relate science to domestic and environmental contexts;
- consider ways in which science is relevant to their health;
- consider how to treat living things and the environment;
- consider how living things and the environment can be protected (Key Stage 2).

3. The nature of scientific ideas
- relate simple scientific ideas to the evidence for them;
- obtain evidence to test scientific ideas in a variety of ways (Key Stage 2);
- recognise that science provides explanations for many phenomena (Key Stage 2).

4. Communication
- use scientific vocabulary;
- present scientific information in a variety of ways;
- use standard measures and SI units appropriate to their work (Key Stage 2);
- use a wide range of methods to present information (Key Stage 2).

5. Health and Safety
- recognise hazards and risks when working with living things and materials;
- follow simple instructions to control the risks to themselves;
- take action to control these risks (Key Stage 2).

SECTIONS OF THE PROGRAMME OF STUDY

The statutory Orders for science are set down in four Sections and the Programme of Study for each Key Stage is set down under each Section. It is intended that teachers will plan from the Programme of Study.

When planning from the Programmes of Study teachers will need to set down clear learning objectives for units of work. The learning objectives should indicate what children should be able to do as a result of being taught a particular unit of work. The learning objectives should be clearly matched to the Programme of Study.

Sc1 Experimental and Investigative Science

This sets down the way in which children should work when undertaking work of an investigative nature.

Contexts for investigative work should derive from work on the other three Sections.

It is recognised that children will not always undertake a full investigation but that the teacher may plan to focus upon specific investigative skills. It is important that teachers teach the skills of scientific investigation as well as providing opportunities for children to apply and practise them.

Please note: The appropriate skills and knowledge need to be taught and learnt before children undertake any scientific investigation.

On some occasions, the whole process of investigating an idea should be carried out by the children themselves.

Sc2 Life Processes and Living Things

At Key Stage 1 this involves the study of plants and animals in the local environment.

At Key Stage 2 this involves the study of plants and animals in the environment. Work on the variety of life in a habitat should be linked to the reasons for classifying living things.

Sc3 Materials and their Properties

At Key Stage 1 this involves the study of the properties of materials and of objects made from them, and the knowledge of the way changes affect the materials.

At Key Stage 2 this involves the study of solids, liquids and gases related to Y4 the changes that take place when materials are heated and cooled, and to ways in which mixtures can be separated. Y6

Sc4 Physical Processes

At Key Stage 1 this involves the study of physical phenomena.

At Key Stage 2 this involves the study of the relationship between forces and motion. It should make clear that both light and vibrations from sound sources travel from the source to a detector. Work on the Earth's place in the solar system should be related to children's knowledge about light.

LEVEL DESCRIPTIONS

Level Descriptions are intended to describe the range of performance that a pupil working at a particular level might be expected to possess or exhibit. They are a description of a pupil and not a particular piece of work.

The Level Descriptions are for teachers to make their end-of-Key Stage assessments against for reporting purposes. They are to be used for making summative judgments at the end of a Key Stage and are not designed for assigning levels to particular pieces of work. However, if teachers are to keep evidence which can support their summative judgment then they will need to look at the Level Descriptions in order to know what they need to make a note of or keep.

Teachers are to be encouraged to use their professional judgment in order to decide which Level Description best describes a particular child rather than ticking off all the separate items within any Level Description.

3   WRITING YOUR SCIENCE POLICY

What to consider when writing your policy

Once the staff have an understanding of what constitutes good science practice and are aware of what the statutory Orders are asking them to cover, it is possible for them to make policy decisions relating to how and when the children will be introduced to the Programmes of Study for science.

Once policy decisions have been made it is easier for schools to identify how and when the various parts of the statutory Orders will be taught.

WHAT MAKES A GOOD POLICY?

A simple guide as to what makes a good policy follows.
1. Keep it short so that people will want to read it.
2. Decide on the readership. For example, governors, teachers, parents, visitors to the school and inspectors.
3. Ensure it is free from unnecessary scientific terminology, especially if it is going to be distributed to parents.
4. A new teacher to the school, or supply teacher should be able to understand fully what is expected.
5. Can you clearly see what you are setting out to achieve and will you be able to identify or measure your success?
Remember that a good policy is a management tool which will assist headteachers in bringing about change in the quality of education within their school.

A good indicator of how well a policy has been prepared and written is to ask whether a visitor to the school could read the policy and, if everybody were teaching science on that day, clearly observe aspects of the policy being addressed, worked towards or set down in the school's long-term plan.

DRAWING UP YOUR SCHOOL SCIENCE POLICY

The following headings form the framework for a school's Science Policy. Staff should be led through a series of staff meetings to address each of the headings and come up with an agreement as to how information should be placed under each.

Under each of the headings there is guidance on what issues might be discussed and suggested statements.

At the end of this section is an example Science Policy which schools might like to use as a guide. Schools may, of course, choose to adapt the example policy to meet their own situation and requirements.

The philosophy of science

What are the areas of knowledge, skills, attitudes and qualities which you feel need to be taught?

How will the general introduction to the Programmes of Study and the Programmes of Study for Attainment Target 1 help you to form a philosophy which promotes good science teaching and learning?

Does what you have written reflect what you agreed earlier was good science teaching?

Science in the national curriculum

Write a short paragraph which introduces the Programme of Study.

When will each aspect of the Orders be covered?

Where will staff go to find out exactly what they are to cover and when?

Has the school drawn up a Programme for Science which sets down exactly when various aspects of the statutory Orders are to be covered at each Key Stage?

How will the children's skills of scientific investigation be developed through the school?

Teaching strategies and planning

What guidance will teachers receive in planning a wide range of investigations and activities which are appropriate to the children's ability, knowledge and skills to be taught?

What approach will staff be required to take to the planning of science investigations and activities?

In the classroom

What organisational strategies will be encouraged in school to develop the children's knowledge, skills and attitudes?

In what ways will children be encouraged to report and record their work?

How will Information Technology be encouraged through the context of scientific investigations and activities?

Equal opportunities and special needs

How will the school ensure that all children are given the same opportunities within their science work?

How will the school provide access for the majority of children as set out in the Common Requirements?

How will teachers plan to ensure that all children are having opportunities to work to their full potential whether it be at the lower levels or at the higher levels?

Assessment and record keeping

How will the school keep a record of when the Programmes of Study have been undertaken?

How will the assessment of science be carried out within the school?

How does the school intend teachers' assessments to inform future planning?

What information are teachers required to keep in order to inform reporting to parents and for end-of-Key Stage assessments?

What guidelines will be given to teachers on the keeping of evidence?

✗ How will reports indicate children's progress and not just provide an account of work undertaken?

Resources   How are the resources to be organised in school?

Are there to be resources kept centrally as well as some in the classrooms?

Is there to be a system adopted for the borrowing and return of central resources?

Will somebody be responsible for ensuring the smooth running of the system and replenishing of stocks?

How will the children be encouraged to use the resources?

 R + L/S   **Early years**   How will the very young children in school be introduced to science and the way of working?

Safety and care   What safety aspects will you want to set down so that all present and future staff are aware of the policies on:
- use of electrical items;
- craft knives;
- experiments with food;
- other issues specific to your school.   *glass items, thermometers,*

How will the school encourage a safe approach in the teaching of science to ensure the well-being of all children involved?

How will the children be encouraged to handle and care for all living things?

→ Where is the Health and Safety Document kept?

Review   How often will you as a school review your policy to update and refine it as appropriate?

HOW WILL THE POLICY SUPPORT SCIENCE TEACHING IN YOUR SCHOOL?

The writing and review of your Science Policy will encourage professional debate and increase the awareness of the staff as to what is required in their teaching.

It will help to develop continuity and progression and give guidance for maintaining and developing quality in teaching and in the children's work.

New members of staff should be able to look at the policy and know what is required of them in their teaching and planning.

It should also guide the headteacher, co-ordinator and any visitors as to what to look for when evaluating the quality of the science teaching taking place in the school.

The curriculum policy for science   The policy must cover the following.
1. Reflect the ideals and philosophy which are promoted in the whole School Curriculum Policy for your school.
2. Reflect the ethos which you hope to create for the teaching of science at your school.

3. Guide the classteacher when planning a wide range of science activities for all children.
4. Help to achieve consistency.
5. Be short and written in a language everyone can understand, i.e. parents and governors.
6. Reflect the work currently being undertaken in the classrooms or what teachers are working towards.
7. Help the classteacher deliver the National Curriculum.

AN EXAMPLE SCIENCE POLICY

For the purpose of this publication we have written a school Science Policy based on the questions outlined on pages 8–9.

This example policy will form the basis around which we will map out the whole of the statutory Orders for science (chapter 5). It will also influence how we will plan our investigations and activities to deliver the Programmes of Study for each Key Stage and it will be represented throughout our Scheme of Work.

The ultimate test of the success of your policy is that it is reflected within the practice that is observed throughout your school.

The philosophy of science	For young children science is an introduction to the world of living things, materials and energy. It is a largely practical subject which develops a spirit of enquiry by encouraging curiosity and reason. Scientists have revealed vast amounts of knowledge about our world by using the skills of observation, prediction, investigation and interpretation. Each child needs to enjoy the experiences associated with science by increasing and developing their knowledge and by starting to use the skills associated with scientific methods of investigation. Working with others, learning how to persevere and learning how to ask questions are attitudes which encourage work to be carried out in a scientific way.
Science in the national curriculum	Each child will be involved in at least one full investigation every term which develops skills to: ■ ask questions, predict and consider apparatus to be used; ■ observe, measure and undertake a fair test; ■ interpret results and evaluate scientific evidence. All children will undertake scientific activities each term throughout Key Stages 1 and 2. The Orders for science have been broken down into units of work. The units of work have been set out in the school's Programme for Science. Each unit of work is made up of a number of related activities that children should undertake prior to tackling the investigations for that unit. The scientific investigations for each unit may need to be adapted to suit the children's abilities and previous experiences. In addition, at Year 6, the children will have one session each week which involves revision and opportunities to recall and extend work from the previous year's Programme.
Teaching strategies and planning	It is important that the teacher identifies the most appropriate teaching strategy to suit the purpose of a particular learning situation.

There are a variety of ways in which the teaching may be effective. Our school has a tradition for encouraging learning through investigation, with an emphasis on firsthand experience. It is, however, frequently acceptable to use demonstration, research, exploration, and teacher-led investigations when circumstances, resources and the needs of individuals and groups allow.

Teachers need to use their flair, enthusiasm, and professional judgement to identify the most sensible, enjoyable and safe methods for the work being conducted. The Scheme of Work provides suggestions to help in the selection of the most effective approach.

In the classroom

Teachers should look for opportunities to praise co-operation and safe, considerate behaviour.

Children are encouraged to work as individuals, in pairs, in groups and also as a whole class when appropriate.

The children are encouraged to use a variety of means for communicating and recording their work. The development of study skills and personal working styles is encouraged and respected. Participating as a speaker and a listener has a high profile at our school.

Information Technology, including computers, tapes and cameras, plays an important role in developing communication and data handling skills. At Key Stage 2 each child will use a computer at least once every half term for data handling and for interpreting results and findings. All the children will maintain a personal data base recording their growth and observations related to living things around the school.

Equal opportunities and special needs

Every effort is made to ensure that science activities and investigations are equally interesting for both boys and girls.

Children with special educational needs are involved in all work planned from the Programme for Science at an appropriate level which will help each child reach their full potential. Teachers' weekly plans show how the activities have been adapted or extended for children of different abilities.

Assessment and record keeping

The Programme for Science indicates the aspects of the Programme of Study to be taught.

Teachers shall set learning objectives for each unit of work to aid their teacher assessments.

Teachers compile individual folders for each child. The folders contain both examples of work which have been assessed and notes relating to observations and conversations with the child.

Every child within the class should be assessed at least once a term by carrying out observations or by collecting written evidence.

Teachers could retain representative samples of class work where it provides support for teachers' assessments.

Resources

Every classroom has access to a resource area. The children are encouraged to choose from a range of equipment when designing investigations. Children are trained in the safe and considerate use of animals, plants and equipment and not to be careless with consumables and materials which are not easy to store.

The Science Co-ordinator is responsible for these areas. Any expensive items which are kept within the central store should be requested from this teacher.

Early years

Reception children should be involved in any science activity which has an appropriate interest value and which has the capacity to excite and provide enjoyment.

The teachers of these very young children are encouraged to plan alongside their Year 1 colleagues and to use the Programme for Science as a structure for identifying activities which the children can undertake.

Safety and care

The safe use of equipment is promoted at all times.

The ASE *Safety Policy* has been adopted by the staff and spare copies are available from the Science Co-ordinator.

The school's Health and Safety policy (available in the staffroom, office and reception area) should be consulted for details regarding scissors, craft knives, electrical equipment, wet areas, heavy equipment and the use of tools.

Any animals, including insects, being used for study should be treated with respect and returned as soon as the activity is complete. For specific guidance related to work undertaken on 'decay' consult the ASE *Safety Policy*.

Leaves and berries of a poisonous nature should be avoided in classroom displays and their dangers made clear to the children.

Review

This policy is reviewed by the staff and governors in the summer term. Parents are most welcome to request this document and comments are invited from anyone involved in the life of the school.

Developing Sc1–Science

Investigations

Sc1 Experimental and Investigative Science

The importance of Sc1

The overall aim of Sc1 is:

> That children are working towards developing the scientific knowledge and skills to enable them to plan, undertake and evaluate scientific investigations.

The challenge facing schools

The challenge facing primary schools is to set down an overall plan for Key Stages 1 and 2 that will provide opportunities for children to develop the appropriate investigative skills. Schools should look to provide activities that develop the scientific skills required to undertake full investigations.

The science skills, as outlined in Sc1, will only be achieved over a period of time and not all children will become totally confident and proficient during their primary education. For children working towards this achievement it is important that primary school staff plan as a team to identify the progression within Sc1 and, from this, plan appropriate scientific activities.

Overall planning for science in primary schools should provide:
■ activities that focus upon specific investigative skills;
■ teacher–directed activities that lead children carefully through a scientific investigation;
■ activities that provide children with the opportunity to take responsibility for a part of the investigation;
■ activities where children take on the full responsibility for the investigation.

The scientific skills

Suggesting ideas that can be investigated

Initially teachers will need to provide suggestions for investigations, and to lead children through the stages of taking the idea and turning it into an investigation. A focus for a short lesson might be a discussion of ideas for investigations and an analysis of why some ideas can and others cannot be investigated.

Children will not automatically come up with ideas that can be investigated without having prior practice and having begun to develop an understanding of what constitutes a scientific investigation. A whole class can be presented with an idea and then led through each stage of an investigation in order to make clear the whole process of undertaking a scientific investigation.

Making predictions

When first asked to make predictions children very often simply make a guess. The guess is not based upon any scientific knowledge nor the analysis or interpretation of any scientific data. Only with practice, and a sound scientific knowledge, will children learn to make predictions that are based upon scientific knowledge and/or data.

Within any primary class teachers may have to plan for a wide range of prediction skills including:
- children making a guess;
- children making a prediction and a reason for their prediction;
- children making a prediction based upon some everyday experience;
- children make a prediction based upon scientific knowledge (which may or may not be correct);
- children make a prediction based upon sound scientific knowledge and understanding.

Teachers should see making predictions as a part of the planning process which acts as an aid to monitoring the progress of an investigation and of knowing what to plan for, rather than being the reason for the investigation.

Controlling factors and undertaking a fair test

Ensuring a 'fair test' is an important aspect of any scientific investigation. The term 'variable' has now been replaced with the term 'factor' to recognise that there are often factors that can affect the outcome of an investigation that are not easily quantified or controlled.

Children's understanding should begin with the fact that investigations need to be 'fair' and progress to children identifying factors and learning to control and change them.

Using scientific equipment

Schools will need to identify the scientific equipment that children are to use within science investigations. Activities may need to be planned to provide children with opportunities to be taught and to practise using specific pieces of equipment.

Primary schools might consider setting down the equipment the majority of children should leave school having used within science lessons. The list may include the following:
- a wide range of observational equipment including strong observational lenses and binocular microscopes;
- a wide range of measuring equipment including thermometers and measuring cylinders;
- a wide range of timers including sand timers and stop clocks;
- specific scientific equipment including magnets and a Newton meter.

All schools will need to ensure that planning for science identifies the use and application of Information Technology. IT equipment might include digital thermometers, digital scales, logging devices for recording light or temperature changes over time or where a CD–Rom could be used for researching a specific aspect of science under study.

Making observations

The skill of making observations, of looking closely and applying all the senses to make sense of the world, needs to be planned for throughout all Key Stages. The observational skills are not applicable to science alone and much work can be undertaken to develop observation and recording skills in art.

Within any primary class teachers may have to plan for a wide range of observational skills including:

■ children make observations based upon an 'overall' picture and 'first impressions';
■ children begin to look more closely at objects, which is reflected in their closer attention to detail, eg: colour in their sketches and drawings;
■ children begin to notice differences and/or similarities between similar objects or events;
■ children can identify patterns in a number of objects, events and/or data;
■ children can observe differences and/or similarities and record their information in the most appropriate manner from a known range.

Measuring

The development of the skills of measuring will be closely linked to work undertaken and achievements in mathematics. Planning within maths should take into consideration the measuring skills required within science.

A school's planning should ensure that, as children develop the basic skills required for taking measurements they are then given opportunities to choose the most appropriate method of measuring. This will require teachers to organise equipment in a way that provides opportunities for children to make a choice of the most appropriate equipment.

As children progress through the school they should be given opportunities to use more sophisticated measuring equipment including types that illustrate the use of Information Technology.

Children should work throughout Key Stages 1 and 2 with increased accuracy in their ability to measure. There will, however, be occasions when measurements cannot easily be made. On these occasions they should be provided with opportunities to observe as carefully as possible. This is set out clearly within the Orders where the word 'measuring' is always followed by 'and/or observations'.

Recording

Children will need to be taught how to record their findings in an appropriate manner. Initially teachers may construct a graph upon which the children place their results. As children progress through the Key Stages they should be developing a wider knowledge of the variety of ways in which results can be recorded and the children's presentations should reflect this. Different methods of recording will have been taught to the children. When analysing results teachers will have questioned the appropriateness of the different ways in which results have been presented. The more able children will be deciding upon the most appropriate way of recording their results from a known range. When making presentations of work undertaken the more able children will have recorded their results in a specific way to make them clearer to others.

Children should have been provided with opportunities to make observations over time, and to draw conclusions from their recordings. For example, this can be undertaken when looking at changes in their body heights throughout the year, or in logging the light changes in their classrooms over a 24 hour period.

Opportunities should be provided for children to use Information Technology applications for recording. This may include a database, a simple graphing program or a data logging program.

Drawing conclusions

Children progress through the following broad stages in their ability to draw conclusions from scientific investigations:
■ children explain what they have undertaken;
■ children say whether what happened was what they expected;
■ children explain their investigation and explain what they have found out;

■ children take account of patterns when they draw conclusions, and begin to relate their conclusions to scientific knowledge and understanding;

■ children explain their investigation and the explanation of their results is related to their prediction;

■ children draw conclusions that are consistent with their evidence and begin to relate these to their scientific knowledge and understanding;

■ children draw conclusions that are consistent with their evidence and explain these using their scientific knowledge and understanding.

TEACHER-ORGANISATION GUIDE

Throughout chapter 6 the majority of investigations have been set down as full investigations covering all the skills listed above.

It is not intended that teachers teach each of the investigations in their entirety. Teachers will need to adapt the investigation to the abilities and previous experiences of the children. It may be that an aspect of the investigation is taught in order to focus upon a single scientific skill. Another teacher may decide to lead the whole class through each stage of the investigation in order to provide the children with a clear understanding of what constitutes a full scientific investigation.

The investigations are broad in that each has been written to a specific Key Stage. They will, particularly at Key Stage 2, where a period of four years has been written for, need to be adapted to suit the age and ability of the children.

To assist teachers in adapting the investigations, or in writing their own, we have compiled questions which teachers will need to consider under each heading when planning their investigation.

Investigation planner

Scientific knowledge What scientific knowledge will the children require in order to undertake the investigation? What scientific activities might they undertake in the investigation?

Teacher question Set the context for the investigation.

Explain your ideas about what the children might investigate.

Ensure the question is open-ended if you wish to encourage the children to devise their own investigation. For example: 'Investigate what things are needed for seeds to grow'.

The question provides opportunities for children to have more control over what they want to investigate – light, water, soil or type of seed.

If the question is closed then the children can make no decisions on what to investigate. For example 'What type of soil is best for growing seedlings?' allows the children only to investigate the type of soil!

The investigation should allow some decisions to be made by the children regarding predicting, questioning and originating ideas.

Resources Decide on the equipment and materials which will be required. Have the children gained experience of using them or will you need to give guidance and instructions or an opportunity to use the equipment before they undertake the investigation?

What equipment will be to hand for children to choose from? Have the children been trained to use the equipment safely and correctly? Teachers need to decide to plan for opportunities for the children to select materials and equipment themselves or to restrict them in their choice.

Starting point It is important that teachers choose suitable starting points which will act as a stimulus to children undertaking the investigation *or* that place it within the context of the children's experience. Build the investigation upon work undertaken in the other three Sections of the Programme of Study.

Observing and asking questions Provide a variety of opportunities to promote discussion between the children, teacher and children, and children and other adults.

The amount of teacher guidance and input will vary considerably depending upon:
- the children's previous experience in undertaking investigations;
- the complexity of the investigation being undertaken;
- the age of the children;
- the general ability of the children;
- the assessments being undertaken.

Teachers may have to sit with children and ask appropriate questions to give children the opportunity to predict in order to assess the different levels of ability within a group.

Teachers should use their professional judgement concerning the amount of input they give.

Give every opportunity to handle, observe and discuss the area being investigated.

At this stage teachers may need to increase the children's knowledge of the area to be investigated.

In writing the investigations due note was given to *Curriculum Organisation in Classroom Practice in Primary Schools: a discussion paper* by Rose and Woodhead, which calls upon teachers to match teaching style to work being undertaken. The main implications of the report for the teaching of scientific investigations are as follows.

1. There are times when it is easier, more effective and time-saving to gather the whole class together to give them information that they are all required to know.
2. There are times when discussions might best be undertaken with a whole class.
3. Children might undertake research, watch a demonstration, explore and discover, or have the teacher explain something to the whole class.

What is important is that the teacher matches the most appropriate approach to the task in hand.

Children may ask Teachers should encourage the children to come up with their own ideas to be investigated.

They cannot ask questions if they have nothing on which to draw and so they should be provided with sufficient stimulus, knowledge and direction to enable them to think of sensible ideas which can be investigated.

The ideas may be verbalised or written down but often children undertake work having already asked themselves the questions. A child may have independently selected two healthy plants and placed them in different conditions of light, for example.

Isolating one factor Most investigations at Key Stage 1 and at Key Stage 2 should direct children to pose questions that allow them to investigate a single factor or variable. When children are undertaking an investigation into the growth of plants, they may plant seeds and place them around the classroom. Some plants thrive, some do not and some do not grow at all. At the end of the half-term the children may be aware that some seeds grow and others do not but have learnt little about the effects of water, light or soil type on the growth of a plant. It is at this stage that the teacher needs to ensure that the children are fully aware of what it is that they are to investigate and observe. It is for the teacher to assist or direct the children in isolating just one factor, for example, water, that affects the growth of plants.

Such an approach, as well as being more effective in developing children's scientific knowledge, will make the investigation easier for the teacher to manage and for the children to undertake. The children will need to be gathered together at regular intervals to explain their work to others so that they are aware of the way others undertake their investigations and gain greater knowledge of the effects of other factors on the growth of plants.

The more able children at Key Stage 2 should be given the opportunity to investigate more than one factor at a time.

Predicting Encourage children to predict what they think will happen in their investigation prior to undertaking it.

To assist teachers in planning and carrying out their assessment it is helpful to see children as progressing through four stages at Key Stages 1 and 2:

Stage 1 **Predicting**
Children make a prediction.

Children may say
I think the more stirs you give it the faster the sugar will disappear.

Stage 2 **Predicting**
Children make a prediction based on an everyday experience.

Children may say
I think the more stirs you give it the faster the sugar dissolves because my Auntie always stirs her tea for a long time to dissolve the sugar quickly.

Stage 3 **Predicting**
Children make a prediction based upon relevant prior knowledge.

Children may say
I think the sugar will dissolve more quickly if placed in hot liquid because when we made jelly it dissolved more quickly in hot water.

Stage 4 **Predicting**
Children make a prediction based upon relevant scientific knowledge.

Children may say
I think when you add sugar to hot water it will dissolve more quickly because the particles move about more quickly when heated.

Designing and planning the investigation Children should be given the opportunity to plan and decide how they are going to undertake the investigation. However, younger and less able children may require significantly more teacher input and guidance.

Once children have decided on their investigations they will need to:
■ identify how they can make their investigation 'fair';
■ decide which factor they are going to change. If they are to investigate the effects of the quantity of water on the growth of plants then they will need to change the quantity of water given to each plant. Everything else in the investigation will need to be kept the same so that the children can see more clearly the results and the teacher can more easily manage the investigation.

Children should be considering the health and safety aspects and care of living things in the investigations they plan.

Teachers should not allow children to proceed further until they are clear exactly what is to be investigated and how the children will carry out their investigation.

Look back at the list of resources

Are there any health and safety aspects that you need to bring to the children's attention?

Are there any aspects of care and consideration for plants, animals and/or others that need to be brought to the children's attention?

Consider the aspects of Information Technology that might be used to assist in the investigations. The following may be considered:
■ making an observational drawing using an art program;
■ presenting data in an appropriate format. For example, pie chart, line graph, scattergram;
■ monitoring changes in temperature or light over a period of time;
■ using a data handling program to interrogate and present data.

Recording

Children should make decisions about how they record their observations and in what form.

In order to make decisions children will need to have had experience in recording using:
■ graphs;
■ charts;
■ databases;
■ diagrams;
■ drawings;
■ close observational drawings;
■ notes.
The method children use for recording should communicate effectively to others the information they have gathered. Set the children the challenge of explaining their findings to others in the clearest possible way.

There should always be a purpose for children's recordings so that they can be used for interpretation and drawing conclusions.

Drawing conclusions

Children should be drawing conclusions based upon what they observed in their investigation.

Conclusions should be based upon the data collected or observations made within the children's investigation and not solely on their original prediction.

Children should comment on whether their investigation was 'fair'. At higher levels children should be giving reasons for their comments and giving guidance on how the investigation could have been improved.

Children should be looking for patterns within the data they have collected.

Children may be reporting on what happened and giving reasons. At this level teachers should be looking for children to be quantifying their results. Instead of saying 'the plant grew 30 cm' children can say 'the plant grew 2 cm every week'.

Summary of skills in Sc1

	Planning experimental work	Obtaining evidence	Considering evidence
Key Stage 1	• Turning ideas into a form that can be investigated • Thinking about what is expected to happen in an investigation • Recognising when a test or comparison is unfair	• Exploring using appropriate senses • Making observations and measurements • Making a record of observations and measurements	• Communicating what happened during the work • Using drawings, tables and bar charts to present results • Making simple comparisons • Using results to draw conclusions • Identifying whether evidence collected supports any prediction made • Explaining what was found drawing on previous knowledge and understanding
Key Stage 2	• Turning ideas into a form that can be investigated • Making predictions • Deciding on evidence to be collected • Changing one factor and observing or measuring the effect whilst keeping other factors the same and knowing that this allows a fair test or comparison to be made • Considering what apparatus and equipment to use	• Using simple apparatus and equipment correctly • Making careful observations and measurements • Checking observations and measurements by repeating them	• Using tables, bar charts and line graphs to present results • Making comparisons and identifying trends or patterns in results • Using results to draw conclusions • Indicating whether evidence collected supports any prediction made • Explaining conclusions in terms of scientific knowledge and understanding

Progression in Sc1

	Planning experimental work	Obtaining evidence	Considering evidence
Level 1		Describe simple features of objects, living things and events they observe.	Communicating findings in simple ways through talking, drawings or simple charts.
Level 2	Children respond to the teacher's suggestions of how to find things out. With help they can make their own suggestions.	Use simple equipment provided and make observations related to their task. Children compare objects, living things and events they observe.	Children describe their observations and record them using simple tables. They say whether what happened was what they expected.
Level 3	Children respond to suggestions, put forward their own ideas and, where appropriate, make simple predictions.	Make relevant observations and measure quantities, such as length or mass, using a range of simple equipment. With some help children carry out a fair test, recognising and explaining why it is fair.	Children record their observations in a variety of ways. They provide explanations for observations and, where they occur, for simple patterns in recorded measurements. They say what they have found out from their work.
Level 4	Children recognise the need for a fair test, describing, or showing in the way they perform their task, how to vary one factor whilst keeping others the same.	Where appropriate, children make predictions. They select suitable equipment to use and make a series of observations and measurements that are adequate for the task.	Children present their observations and measurements clearly, using tables and bar charts. They begin to plot points to form simple graphs and use these to point out and interpret patterns or trends in their data. They take account of these patterns when drawing conclusions, and begin to relate these to scientific knowledge and understanding.
Level 5	Children identify key factors they need to consider in contexts that involve only a few factors. Where appropriate, they make predictions based on their scientific knowledge and understanding	Children select apparatus for a range of tasks and use it with care. They make a series of observations and measurements with precision appropriate to the task.	Children begin to repeat observations and measurements and to offer simple explanations for any differences they encounter. They record observations and measurements systematically and present data as line graphs. They draw conclusions that are consistent with the evidence and begin to relate these to scientific knowledge and understanding.

Guiding teacher's planning

The following information is provided to help teachers to focus on the various stages that children may work through when undertaking a full scientific investigation. The order the children work through the stages will vary according to the investigation being undertaken.

Children should be given the opportunity to work through a full investigation, from deciding what to investigate to analysing and evaluating results. However, investigative work can be undertaken without taking children through the full process. The teacher may, for instance, plan and organise an investigation for a whole class and then invite the children to interpret the results in order to develop specific investigative skills.

The following is designed to assist teachers in keeping 'on track', in ensuring that the activity remains an investigation and in helping to identify opportunities for undertaking assessments.

Before the investigation

1. What do you want to find out in your investigation?
   or
   How might you turn the teacher's suggested idea into an investigation?

2. How will you undertake your investigation?
   ■ How will you make your investigation 'fair'?
   ■ What factor are you going to change?
   ■ Where will you undertake your investigation?
   ■ What equipment are you going to use?
   ■ Is your investigation safe?
   ■ What evidence will you need to gather together?

3. What do you think will happen?
   Can you give a reason for your prediction?

4. How will you record your findings?

5. Carry out the investigation.

6. What happened in your investigation?

After the investigation

7. Was your investigation 'fair'?

8. Can you explain why you think it happened?
   Can you explain what happened using scientific knowledge and understanding?

9. If you did the investigation again what would you do differently?

5 DRAWING UP A PROGRAMME FOR SCIENCE

Mapping the science curriculum

Once the policy is written schools will need to map out within a Programme for Science exactly how and when the various Sections of the statutory Orders for science are to be taught. This will help teachers in their planning, enable headteachers to monitor coverage and aid the development of progression throughout the school.

The policy decisions you have made will allow you to establish how many times and when the children will experience the various aspects of the Orders, and how your school will be approaching the teaching of the scientific skills of Sc1.

Many schools will now have existing plans for science and these can be incorporated or adapted into a school Programme for Science.

AN EXAMPLE PROGRAMME FOR SCIENCE

The example Programme for Science has been set out to reflect the statements set down in the example Science Policy.

The example Programme for Science shows which classes in the school will address the different aspects of the Orders.

It could be used by any school irrespective of the number of classes. However, where mixed age groups are taught the school may well have to adapt the simplistic format shown here to a two- or three-year cycle.

It could be used whatever the organisation of year groups within classes or whatever the elected style of delivery (subject or topic based).

UNITS OF WORK

The Orders for science have been broken down into units of work. Each unit of work contains a number of activities that together cover the relevant aspects of a Section of the Programme of Study. These aspects are clearly indicated at the start of each unit.

There are 7 units of work for Key Stage 1 and 12 units for Key Stage 2. Together the units ensure full coverage of the Orders for science.

Each unit of work, except unit 5 at Key Stage 1, contains a full scientific investigation. The investigation draws upon the knowledge gained from having undertaken the activities for that unit. The investigations should only be undertaken after the activities set down have been taught. The activities provide the skills and knowledge to equip the children in tackling the investigation.

The investigation for each unit may have to be adapted by teachers. The investigation may need to be altered to better match the age and experiences of the children. The teacher may decide to tackle a part of the investigation in order to focus on tackling specific scientific skills.

It is not intended that the investigations are undertaken entirely by the children. Teachers will need to decide on the degree of guidance provided. There are times when a teacher may lead the whole class through an investigation in order to develop an understanding of the main elements of the scientific process.

Schools will need to decide when each unit of work is to be taught within a Key Stage. The following may assist schools in deciding when each will be taught:

- a school may decide that every class will undertake a unit of work from each Section of the Programme of Study – 'Life Processes and Living Things', 'Materials and their Properties' and 'Physical Processes';
- it may be advantageous for all the school to tackle units of work from the same Section of the Programme of Study each term. In this way the whole school is undertaking related activities that all children and staff can observe. This approach can, however, make great demands for the same equipment and materials such that a school may be unable to resource it;
- where plants are grown and observed within a unit of work the most appropriate term will need to be chosen;
- where a Year 6 class undertakes work on Health or Sex Education it may be advantageous for them to be undertaking the unit of work best matched to support their work in these areas;
- a specific educational visit may be well-suited to a particular unit of work;
- a teacher's expertise or interest may well decide who teaches a particular unit of work;
- there may be less time available in certain terms for a particular year group. In this case it may be appropriate to undertake a unit of work that makes less demands on their time.

An example Programme for Science has been set out for each Key Stage on the following pages.

Key Stage 1: Programme for Science

	Autumn term	Spring term	Summer term
Y1	**Unit 2** **Life Processes and Living Things** 2. Humans as organisms 4. Variation and classification	**Unit 4** **Materials and their Properties** 2. Changing materials	**Unit 6** **Physical Processes** 2. Forces and motion
Y2	**Unit 3** **Materials and their Properties** 1. Grouping materials	**Unit 7** **Physical Processes** 3. Light and sound	**Unit 1** **Life Processes and Living Things** 1. Life processes 3. Green plants as organisms 5. Living things in their environment

Note: Teachers are advised that unit 5 – Electricity – is best taught within a Design and Technology project.

Key Stage 2: Programme for Science

	Autumn term	Spring term	Summer term
Y3	**Unit 11** **Physical Processes** 3. Light and sound	**Unit 3** **Life Processes and Living Things** 3. Green plants as organisms	**Unit 6** **Materials and their Properties** 1. Grouping and classifying materials
Y4	**Unit 9** **Physical Processes** 1. Electricity	**Unit 4** **Life Processes and Living Things** 4. Variation and classification	**Unit 7** **Materials and their Properties** 2. Changing materials
Y5	**Unit 12** **Physical Processes** 4. The Earth and beyond	**Unit 5** **Life Processes and Living Things** 5. Living things in their environment	**Unit 8** **Materials and their Properties** 3. Separating mixtures of materials
Y6	**Unit 10** **Physical Processes** 2. Forces and motion	**Unit 1** **Life Processes and Living Things** 1. Life processes	**Unit 2** **Life Processes and Living Things** 2. Humans as organisms (My body or Health Education links)

USING THE PROGRAMME FOR SCIENCE TO PRODUCE YOUR OWN SCHEME OF WORK

The example Programme for Science forms the basis of the Scheme of Work in the following chapter.

There are three possible ways in which schools may use this chapter.
1. Schools may use the example Programme for Science and its associated Scheme of Work directly.
2. Schools may choose to adapt the Programme for Science to produce a Scheme of Work which is directly related to the particular situation of the school.
3. Schools may work through the stages identified and use the guidance provided to produce their own unique Programme for Science and an associated Scheme of Work.

6   Producing your Scheme of Work

Planning investigations and activities

Once a Programme for Science is available the teachers can use it as a foundation to plan a range of investigations and activities which will deliver and introduce all of the Programmes of Study to the children in their class.

WHAT SHOULD BE USED TO HELP IN PLANNING?

Teachers should always use the Programmes of Study as their starting point for planning. These are the learning experiences to which every child should be introduced. The Attainment Targets should be used alongside the Programmes of Study to inform the teacher as to what the children should know or be able to do once they have been introduced to the Programmes of Study.

When planning investigations teachers should ensure that the investigation involves the children working through the whole process as identified by the three strands of Sc1 – Planning experimental work, Obtaining evidence and Considering evidence. This will encourage the children to develop good practice in the carrying out of investigations, and to work in a logical manner.

WHICH TEACHING METHODS SHOULD BE USED?

There is not just one approach to the teaching of science. The teacher needs to make decisions about the most effective way of undertaking particular aspects of the Programme of Study while taking into account the needs of the children.

Different methods will include children being involved in investigations, exploration, demonstration, teacher-led investigation and research. It is expected that there will be a balance between the variety of teaching methods and on many occasions they will work together to provide the best learning experiences for children.

It is apparent, however, that no one technique in isolation can deliver the whole Programme of Study for science.

WHAT ORGANISATIONAL METHODS SHOULD BE USED?

The three main ways of organisation of the learning experiences for children in the classroom are: individual, group or whole class teaching. Teachers should be aiming for a balance of all three, as they all have a role within the teaching of science.

Individual teaching is ideal for the child who needs particular attention to help them develop understanding of a particular concept or to use a particular skill. There are times when whole class teaching may be needed when the teacher wishes to give information. Group work is very appropriate in the development of co-operative learning.

THE IMPORTANCE OF INVESTIGATIONS

Whilst it is very important for teachers to realise that there is not just one way of teaching science it is equally important for teachers to recognise the significance of children being involved in investigations.

The example policy and Programme for Science identify the fact that every child will undertake at least one investigation every term. This is a very important point to which attention should be drawn.

The skills associated with the development of Sc1 can be undertaken through a variety of approaches but it is only through the context of an investigation that the children have the opportunity to work through the whole process of asking questions, making predictions, planning and carrying out the investigation, recording their findings and drawing conclusions.

THE SCHEME OF WORK

For the purpose of this publication we have planned a Scheme of Work based on the Programme for Science found in chapter 5. Pages 31–162 contain investigations and activities which will help teachers deliver the Programmes of Study to the children at Key Stages 1 and 2.

The pathway through the pages is as follows:
1. Each year and term is identified, followed by the unit to be covered in that term.
2. The Programme of Study and what children should be taught are identified for Key Stage 1.
3. A set of activities followed by an investigation which could be used to deliver the unit.
This format is repeated for Key Stage 2.

This chapter therefore contains a complete Scheme of Work which includes activities and investigations suitable for children progressing through Key Stages 1 and 2.

Key Stage 1: Programme for Science

The Orders for Key Stage 1 have been conveniently divided up into 7 units of work. This means that there is one unit of work for each term at Key Stage 1 with unit 5 – Electricity – being taught within a Design and Technology project.

Each unit of work, except unit 5, which does not lend itself to a science investigation, has a scientific investigation included.

Schools can take the units of work and add or adapt as they think fit in the knowledge that, if all are taught at Key Stage 1, then the statutory requirements will be met and children will have covered the appropriate work, and that teachers will be able to undertake assessments at the end of the Key Stage.

To assist schools in planning the coverage of science at Key Stage 1 an example Programme for Science has been included. In the example are set out the terms in which each unit will be taught. Schools may find it helpful to know the criteria used when setting out the example Programme of Science provided.

The units of work for Key Stage 1 were mapped out across Years 1 and 2 after consideration of the following criteria:

- that unit 5 does not lend itself to a scientific investigation and is therefore best planned for within a Design and Technology activity;
- that unit 2 was planned to include a range of activities that provided children with opportunities to practice specific investigative skills. The investigation was written to aid teachers' planning and organisation when working with children at the start of Key Stage 1;
- that units 1 and 2 contain more work than the other units. Related areas have been combined to give the work a relevant focus for the term. The work to be covered will require a full term where major commitments are at a minimum;
- that unit 1 is about growth and plants and therefore needs to be undertaken in the Summer Term;
- that, for the Year 2 teacher, the Spring Term has a great many commitments, particularly with assessment. Therefore unit 7 has been planned for this term as it has less content than some of the other units;
- that all children will undertake a scientific investigation each term;
- that in each year children will cover work within each of the three Attainment Targets.

Key Stage 1: The units of work

Unit 1	Life Processes and Living Things	1. Life processes 3. Green plants as organisms 5. Living things in their environment
Unit 2	Life Processes and Living Things	2. Humans as organisms 4. Variation and classification
Unit 3	Materials and their Properties	1. Grouping materials
Unit 4	Materials and their Properties	2. Changing materials
Unit 5	Physical Processes	1. Electricity
Unit 6	Physical Processes	2. Forces and motion
Unit 7	Physical Processes	3. Light and sound

Key Stage 1: Programme for Science

	Autumn term	Spring term	Summer term
Y1	**Unit 2** **Life Processes and Living Things** 2. Humans as organisms 4. Variation and classification	**Unit 4** **Materials and their Properties** 2. Changing materials	**Unit 6** **Physical Processes** 2. Forces and motion
Y2	**Unit 3** **Materials and their Properties** 1. Grouping materials	**Unit 7** **Physical Processes** 3. Light and sound	**Unit 1** **Life Processes and Living Things** 1. Life processes 3. Green plants as organisms 5. Living things in their environment

Note: Teachers are advised that unit 5 – Electricity – is best planned to be taught within a Design and Technology project.

LIFE PROCESSES AND LIVING THINGS

1. LIFE PROCESSES
3. GREEN PLANTS AS ORGANISMS
5. LIVING THINGS IN THEIR ENVIRONMENT

LIFE PROCESSES AND LIVING THINGS

> Work on life processes should be related to pupils' knowledge of animals and plants in the local environment.

Pupils should be taught:

1. Life processes

a the differences between things that are living and things that have never been alive;

b that animals, including humans, move, feed, grow, use their senses and reproduce.

3. Green plants as organisms

a that plants need light and water to grow;

b to recognise and name the leaf, flower, stem and root of flowering plants;

c that flowering plants grow and produce seeds which, in turn, produce new plants.

5. Living things in their environment

a that there are different kinds of plants and animals in the local environment;

b that there are differences between local environments and that these affect which animals and plants are found there.

SCIENCE ACTIVITIES

Before setting up the investigation, children will need to have undertaken the following activities. The activities provide the children with the opportunity to acquire the skills and knowledge they will require in order to undertake the investigation. Preparing children with the appropriate skills and knowledge will assist the teacher's organisation of the investigation.

Whilst the children are undertaking the activities the teacher should plan to develop a vocabulary with which the children can work.

ACTIVITIES

Life processes

 LIVED OR NEVER LIVED

RESOURCES

An informative class display showing things that have lived and those that have not

Class discussion

Discuss with the class things that are alive and things that have never been alive. Encourage the children to explain how they know if something has lived. Ask them to explain what the differences are between things that are alive now and things that are not alive.

Once you feel the children understand what is meant by 'been alive' and 'not been alive' then ask them to each bring in something from each category. Explain that they must not bring along anything that is alive – or you may be overrun with animals! They can bring along objects or photographs of objects.

Classroom display

Make a classroom display from the things the children bring into school. Once the display is complete discuss with the whole class if everything is in the correct category. You may want to make a list of the criteria the children used to help them check if their objects had lived or not.

2 LOOKING AFTER THE CLASS PET

RESOURCES

A class pet

Children can be given responsibility for looking after a class pet over a period of time. A list can be drawn up of the things that the monitors will have to do to ensure that the pet lives a safe and healthy life.

Once all the children have had responsibility for looking after the pet they will be able to explain some of the things that animals do that are similar to humans. Focus the children's attention on explaining the things that they have all observed when looking after their pet. These will include how their pet moves, feeds, grows and uses its senses.

If teachers do not wish to take on the long term commitment of keeping an animal in the classroom then they can look to purchasing a 'Butterfly Garden School Kit.' This kit allows children to look closely in the classroom at the stages of the life history of the Painted Lady butterfly. The specially designed kit called The Butterfly Garden comes complete with caterpillars, and vials to keep them in, for a class of thirty.

You can observe the caterpillars shedding their skins and hanging from the lid of the vial. Eventually the butterfly emerges and feeds upon the sugar solution supplied. The adult butterflies can be released into the wild.

The life history is over in three to four weeks so making an ideal half-term study.

The Butterfly Garden Kit can be purchased from:

Insect Lore Europe
Suite 6
Linford Forum
Linford Wood
Milton Keynes MK14 6LY

3 A VISIT TO LOOK AT THE ANIMALS

RESOURCES A class visit

The class could go on a visit to observe other animals being looked after. This may be a farm or fishery where children can compare the similarities between the way that they looked after their class pet and how these animals are looked after. There will be opportunities to bring to the children's attention that all animals reproduce.

ACTIVITIES Green plants as organisms

1 PARTS OF A PLANT

RESOURCES A collection of plants for children to examine closely

Teacher demonstration The teacher shows the children a flowering plant such as a daffodil or tulip and identifies the leaf, flower, stem and root. Children could then take a similar plant and draw in detail the parts identified. This could be done for a variety of plants. Children should be encouraged to look for similarities and differences between different plants.

2 HEALTHY PLANTS

RESOURCES Seedlings and plants

Teacher discussion Make a collection of plants including seedlings. Ask the children how you should look after them. What do they need in order to stay healthy? Develop an understanding of what makes a plant healthy and how you would recognise that a plant is unhealthy.

Practical Set out a task rota so the children can take responsibility for the plants. Each week look at how the plants are faring. Look for any signs that the plants are not healthy and ask the children what they might do to improve their condition.

This activity sets the foundations for the investigation at the end of this unit of work. It is important therefore that the children have begun to establish an understanding that plants require light, water, warm temperatures and soil in order to grow healthy. They also need to know and be able to recognise a healthy and unhealthy plant. In order to establish a good understanding of what constitutes a healthy plant some plants may be placed in a cold place or deprived of water so the children can observe the effect of each on plant growth.

3 SEEDS

RESOURCES

A collection of seeds or fruits which can be opened to view seeds inside. (Good examples are: thistle, poppy, sunflower, dandelion, acorns and conkers)

Class or group discussion

Discussion could centre around what plants the seeds come from and what is their purpose.

Practical

The children could observe closely and make drawings of the seeds. Children find out how the seeds are transported and why. The most important aspect of this activity is to develop an understanding that most plants rely on their seeds to ensure the survival of their kind. The children could investigate seeds that are dispersed by wind, for example dandelion seeds. At the end of the activity the seeds could be planted to see how long they take to germinate.

ACTIVITIES

Living things in the environment

Teachers do not have to plan to cover all the activities numbered 1–7 in this section. A selection of activities have been set down for schools to choose those that best suit their situation and environment. Teachers should plan activities that develop children's understanding 'that there are differences between local environments and that these affect which animals and plants are found there'.

 MINIBEAST HABITATS

RESOURCES

A collection of minibeasts from school grounds

Practical

Observe the creatures in the collection through magnifying glasses. Make sketches of them, recording carefully their shape and colour. Look closely at how their bodies are put together, and how they move.

Carry out some research work to find out more information about the creatures that have been observed and why they live where they do.

 PLANT HABITATS

Starting point

Walk outside school and identify different plants growing in different places.

Children are encouraged to explore different habitats around the school, for example, walls, trees and playgrounds. They could note and try to identify different plants growing in the habitats they explore. The children could draw or photograph plants they found. If at first the children cannot identify the plants, suggest they give them a name which they think suits them. Once back in the classroom, identify missing names and produce reference books about the plants found. Encourage the children to question why the plants are living there.

3 THE BIRD TABLE

RESOURCES A bird table, or feeding area

Deciding on the most suitable location for a bird table and its design is likely to create considerable interest in the project amongst the class.

Practical The children could investigate which foods different birds like.

Learning the names of common birds could be encouraged with reference material and by the children sharing their own knowledge. Binoculars and sketching materials left near the observation area could encourage a routine for noting behaviour and characteristics.

How are birds different according to their size, colour, beaks, feet and feeding habits?

These classifications could result in the children making their own charts based on firsthand observations.

The number of birds visiting the feeding area could be recorded and graphs or frequency charts drawn to represent the data. Areas around the school where birds appear to congregate could be identified.

Children could be encouraged to reason why certain localities have a large bird population and some a smaller population.

The RSPB is pleased to send a free teacher's pack with many ideas for bird study projects and other resources. Copies can be obtained from:

The Education Department
Royal Society for the Protection of Birds
The Lodge
Sandy
Bedfordshire SG19 2DL
Tel: 01767 80551

4 THE WILD AREA

RESOURCES A wild area in the school grounds

Practical Designate an area at school 'wild'. Ensure that the area is notified to the groundspeople – once established it will provide a great deal of interest in comparing the area to mown and weeded parts of the grounds. What are the differences? Which living things can be found in the wild area that cannot be found in other parts of the school? Wild flowers could be sown. Get an 'expert' to come into school to offer advice on suitable wild flowers to sow.

5 CHANGES IN OUR ENVIRONMENT

RESOURCES A collection of photographs of a piece of land, in the country or a city, taken over a period of time

Practical The children are encouraged to identify any differences in the photographs. They should try and give reasons for why these changes have occurred.

Wherever possible the children should be encouraged to consider the effects that the changes have had on the wildlife in the area under study. Children should express how they feel about the changes that have been made. These discussions and observations are particularly relevant in city areas and also where hedgerows have been removed in agricultural parts of the countryside.

Encourage children to collect information on changes made to the environment in other parts of the world.

6 STUDYING LOCAL HABITATS

RESOURCES A tree or a length of hedge or an area of wasteland

Children discover what creatures live in these habitats – through firsthand experience supported by research.

What effects would the removal of these habitats have on the wildlife in that area?

Children will be amazed at the amount of wildlife that can be supported by a mature tree or a length of hedge.

What happens to the wildlife once the tree or hedge is removed?

7 A POND DIP

RESOURCES Suitable equipment for carrying out a pond dip

The teacher will need to show the children how to carry out a pond dip and to explain that it can endanger wildlife in the pond if performed incorrectly. Ponds should not be dipped when animals are hibernating.

Careful supervision of all children during a pond dip is important. Suitable clothing is required, and careful plans should be made before the visit. A preliminary visit by the teacher is a good idea to find out what might be found, possible dangers and where children can make safe dips.

Children can find out about the wildlife that lives around the pond as well.

Look at the plants as well as the creatures living in, on and around the pond. Dip into the pond to find any living creatures. Is there a pattern as to where the creatures live – position in the pond – shallow, deep, middle, edge, shady, open? Observe the animals that are found closely. How do they move?

Look for signs of human effects on the pond. What could be done about them and how does it affect the living things that are there?

When the children return to the classroom they can use reference material to make displays of the things they have found. The children could also make large models of the animals they have found based upon their drawings and sketches.

In all these activities the teacher should aim to develop the children's understanding and knowledge of how human activity affects habitats. This should be an underlying message in activities 1–7.

INVESTIGATION Living things in the environment

"Do plants need light in order to grow?"

Resources
- packets of broad beans
- soil or compost
- seed trays or plant pots
- water
- measuring jugs of water
- scales for weighing the compost
- rulers for measuring depth of seeds

Starting point
Before undertaking this investigation it is important that the children have developed an understanding of what makes a plant healthy. They should, for instance, be aware that a plant that is healthy is green. Children who have not developed such an understanding may well consider the plant kept in the dark to be healthier because it is longer.

Observing and asking questions
Read the instructions on the seed packets and discuss the best way of planting the broad beans. Look at healthy plants and ask the children why they think they are healthy. Remind them of how they looked after plants in the classroom (see activity 2 – Healthy plants).

Encourage the children to suggest which aspect of plant care they might investigate. In this case they are going to focus on the effect of light on the growth of the broad beans.

What do they think will happen to the beans which are kept in the light and in the dark? Keep a record of the children's predictions so that they can look back at them at the end and compare their results with what they initially said would happen.

Children may suggest:
The plants in the light will grow best because the ones we looked after had light all the time.

The plants will grow best in the light because they need light to help them make food.

The investigation
When the children are clear about what to investigate, encourage them to decide which things they are going to change and which things they are going to keep the same.

Encourage the children to come up with ways of ensuring that the investigation is fair by ensuring each seed receives the same conditions (depth of soil, temperature, amount of water, planting container) as every other, apart from the amount of light.

The children will select the equipment they will need in order to carry out the investigation. The teacher will offer support and guidance and show them how to use measuring instruments where necessary.

The children need to decide how they will judge whether the seeds are growing successfully or not, for example:
They will be straight and green like the ones we looked after in the classroom.

Teacher tip: It is advisable to plant a number of seeds at the same time and to explain to the children that some may not grow at all. Don't rely upon planting only two seeds.

Recording
The plants could be measured using standard or non-standard measures. Decide on the form of recording – tables, graphs, drawings, or a database.

Information Technology may be used to help the children record their results or in making observations. Data handling packages such as *Data Sweet* (Archimedes), or an art package such as *Flare* could be used for making drawings of the plants at each stage of growth.

Children can make drawings at regular intervals and place them in a booklet. At the end of the investigation they can look back at their drawings and be encouraged to explain what they observed at each stage.

Encourage children to observe and measure accurately and record carefully.

Drawing conclusions

Children should be encouraged to look carefully at their results and try to explain what has happened, rather than simply reporting what happened. Wherever possible encourage children to relate their findings to their original predictions.

Assessment

ATTAINMENT TARGET 1

Set out below are suggestions of the relevant observations you might make at levels 1 to 3 whilst the children are undertaking this investigation.

at level 1
- The children identified that the plant in the dark was longer and white compared to the plant in the light.
- The children made a sketch of the growth of the beans at regular intervals.
- They explained what they did to set up the investigation.
- By looking at the set of drawings that they made throughout the investigation they could point out some of their observations.

at level 2
- The children responded to the question 'How can we find out if plants grow best in the dark or the light?' They made suggestions for undertaking the investigation and, with help from the teacher, could plan their investigation.
- The children could measure and record the growth of the plants using standard or non-standard measures. The children were able to make simple observations as the investigation developed. They could, for instance, observe that the plants were growing at different rates and that the colour of each was different.
- The children undertook the investigation once the teacher had explained what to do and ensured that they knew what they were going to investigate. They suggested ways in which the investigation might be changed.
- The children measured the plants carefully and recorded their growth as a block graph to show how they had grown each week.
- At the end of the investigation the children were able to read their original predictions and explain whether what they had predicted was what happened or not.

at level 3
- The children made simple predictions about which plants would grow to be healthy. They sometimes suggested ways in which the plant would be affected: that it would have fewer leaves, be longer or shorter or that it would never have flowers.
- The plants were carefully measured and recorded over a period of time. Growth was recorded as a graph or by using a simple database which printed out a graph of the plants' growth.
- The children, with help from the teacher, undertook a fair test. They explained how they had placed tape around the cupboard to ensure that the light from around the door would not affect their investigation. Others ensured that each plant received the exact same amount of water at the same time each week. When setting up the investigation children ensured that the same containers were used and the same amount of compost placed in each.
- The children explained what they had found out. They used their recordings to explain what had happened at each stage of the investigation.

LIFE PROCESSES AND LIVING THINGS

2. HUMANS AS ORGANISMS
4. VARIATION AND CLASSIFICATION

LIFE PROCESSES AND LIVING THINGS

Work on life processes should be related to pupils' knowledge of animals and plants in the local environment.

Pupils should be taught:

2. Humans as organisms

a   to name the main external parts, *eg hand*, *elbow*, *knee*, of the human body;

b   that humans need food and water to stay alive;

c   that taking exercise and eating the right types and amount of food help humans to keep healthy;

d   about the role of drugs as medicines;

e   that humans can produce babies and these babies grow into children and then into adults;

f   that humans have senses which enable them to be aware of the world around them.

4. Variation and classification

a   to recognise similarities and differences between themselves and other pupils;

b   that living things can be grouped according to observable similarities and differences.

SCIENCE ACTIVITIES

Before setting up the investigation, children will need to have undertaken the following activities. The activities provide the children with the opportunity to acquire the skills and knowledge they will require in order to undertake the investigation. Preparing children with the appropriate skills and knowledge will assist the teacher's organisation of the investigation.

Whilst the children are undertaking the activities the teacher should plan to develop a vocabulary with which the children can work.

ACTIVITIES

Humans as organisms

PARTS OF THE BODY

RESOURCES	An outline or model of the human body
Class or group discussion	The children play a game of either placing labels on the 'body' showing the main external parts, for example arms, legs, head (and associated features), feet, etc. Or the teacher places labels on the body incorrectly and asks the children to put them in the correct places. Children should not simply be able to say where different parts of the body are but should be encouraged to explain and investigate their functions in a simple way.
Classroom display	Make a classroom display by making an outline of the human body from different materials. Make labels for the different parts of the body. Add Velcro to the backs of the labels so that children can place them in the correct place on the display.

THE BABY

RESOURCES	A visit from a parent and baby, photographs of the baby showing clearly the changes that have taken place as it has grown older
Class or group discussion	Discussion could take place about why humans have babies. Children talk about the baby and how it has changed since it was born (useful to have photographs of the baby at an earlier age). Discuss and write about the daily routines and needs of a baby. How do the needs of the baby compare with older children and adults, or even elderly people?
	Discuss how the baby will change in appearance over the years. Children could compare how they have changed over the years – use old photographs. If birth weights and lengths are available, children could find out if the longest baby is now the tallest child etc.
RESOURCES	It would be interesting to have a collection of pictures of animals and their young: mammals, insects, reptiles etc., and encourage the children to find out about how the young develop and are looked after by their parents

MOVEMENT

Cross-curricular links PHYSICAL EDUCATION	Children during a physical education lesson are encouraged to show movement in a variety of ways, running, jumping, skipping, rolling etc.

Describe which parts of the body are used when they move – and are all these parts used whatever the type of movement, for example running, jumping etc.? Children could then discuss how their bodies feel when they move or do exercise.

Children could collect pictures of various athletes and sports people involved in movement. They could be introduced to the idea of muscles, bones and joints helping us move.

Extension   Children could find out about how children and adults without arms and legs cope with their handicaps and could be encouraged to consider how these people can improve the quality of their everyday lives.

 SENSES

RESOURCES   Set up an 'interest' table with a collection of materials and equipment that encourage the children to use their senses. Collect objects that children can describe by smelling and feeling. Be careful about placing objects on the table that children will have to taste

Sound   Children play a game in which they are blindfolded – sounds made – can the child guess what the sound is?

A sound from a different direction – can the child indicate which direction the sound is coming from?

Tape recordings of sounds around the home – can they be identified?

Sight   Set up an eyesight test so that children can test their own sight and learn how distance affects how well they can see and recognise features. Does it make a difference which eye they look through? Is it better to use both eyes? What difference does it make when they only look through one eye?

Taste and smell   Children play guessing games to see if they can recognise different materials by using just taste and/or smell.

Touch   Mystery object sack. Children play the game – by putting their hands in the sack and telling each other what they can feel. Look closely to see what parts of the hands are used for touching. Children could create a 'feely board' of pleasant objects to touch – children describe why they like to touch the objects.

 KEEPING OURSELVES CLEAN

RESOURCES   A collection of items used to keep ourselves clean

Class discussion   Why is it important to keep clean?

Children discuss what things we use to keep us clean and tidy and how and where these things are used. Pose questions about the need to keep ourselves clean.

Practical   Are there parts of the body that get dirtier than others? Children could investigate which soap is best for washing hands. Does the temperature of water make any difference when washing – try cold water, hot water.

KEEPING OURSELVES FIT

RESOURCES A collection of sporting pictures and sports equipment

Class discussion What sports are the pieces of equipment designed for? The children could discuss the reasons why people play sport. A survey could be carried out throughout school to find out which is the most played sport in school.

How do you feel after exercise? How does your body react to exercise? Discussion could be based around heart beat, breathing rate, temperature. The children should have explained to them in simple terms what is happening in the body during exercise.

Practical The children could investigate heart rate/breathing rate after certain types of exercise.

Children keep a diary of time spent exercising and time spent resting.

MEDICINES

RESOURCES *George's Marvellous Medicine* by Roald Dahl

Class discussion Discuss with the children why we have medicines. What type of illnesses have medicines been taken for in your class? Discuss the safe use of medicines – why is it important?

ACTIVITIES Variation and classification

LOOKING AT MINIBEASTS

RESOURCES This activity is easier to undertake if the school has an environmental area. Children will need to have access to the correct equipment for collecting and observing minibeasts. Collect observation containers, magnifiers, hand lenses and an old fish tank or shoe boxes for creating suitable environments

Class discussion The children could be asked to share their knowledge of where minibeasts are to be found around the school and in their neighbourhood. A class discussion could also invite the children to consider places where they think similar creatures might be found and to talk about the conditions which they seem to favour.

Where can we find insects around the school? Under stones, bark, walls and hedges? Observe them carefully in their environment.

Do they all like living in the same places?
How do they move?
What special features can you see? How do they protect themselves?
How do you think they see, hear, smell and feel?

How could you collect these creatures? How must they be handled? How are they to be treated if we are going to look at them closely?

When observed closely we need to be looking for differences and similarities between the animals in the collection.

Do you know the proper names for some of these animals?
Use reference books to help us find out the names of others.

The children could also make up names for individual or groups of insects. This would help the children appreciate the classification of animals into species and encourage close observation. Ask the children to classify the creatures according to observable features, for example, number of legs, colour and ways of moving.

Practical Drawing the animals and recording the place where each animal was discovered may help the children identify further places inhabited by a particular type of insect.

Do all little creatures like the same conditions?

Which of the creatures appear to prefer damp, dark places? (Woodlice are ideal for young children to observe and study.)

The children should be encouraged to devise simple investigations to test their ideas. A simple environment with contrasting areas of damp and light will help to confirm some of the predictions raised in the class or group discussion.

The children might then create a home for woodlice, in an old shoe box or something similar, in the classroom based on the knowledge which they have gained.

The importance of care and safe return of all animals after a short period of study should be stressed.

2 TREES

RESOURCES Trees and shrubs

Practical Groups or individuals could adopt a tree or some shrubs within the school grounds, at home, or in the immediate locality of the school and start a diary containing brief observations and comments made over a long period of time. (The data could be kept on a child's personal data disk and be updated at regular intervals during their time at the school.)

The children could examine the leaves of the tree and consider how they are similar or different to those on plants.

The bark, branches and shape of the tree could be examined and the children could record the colours and texture of the tree. Leaves could be picked to press in work books. Measurements, photographs, sketches and written observations should all be added to the diary to record the seasonal changes and growth of the tree.

How often will you return to look for changes on the tree?
How will you show your findings?
How could you inform the other children about your observations?
Are there other plants which appear to change in similar ways? Which other shrubs and trees appear to change little between the seasons?

Ask the children to group the plants they have observed according to observable features such as whether they shed their leaves in winter, the shape of the leaves and the way the leaves are arranged on the branches.

WHERE PLANTS GROW

Practical Looking at plants around the school.

Where can plants be found around our school? Are there any plants growing in unusual places (in walls, between paving stones)?

How might they have been planted?
Why do they seem to grow quite well in these places?
Which places around school seem difficult for plants to grow? Can you suggest reasons why?

4 **DINOSAURS**

RESOURCES A collection of model dinosaurs

The collection gives the opportunity to ask the children to identify the differences and similarities with creatures living today.

Many children will know and be keen to offer the names of the dinosaurs.

Class discussion The discussion should introduce the term 'extinct'.

The fact that these creatures lived so long ago may need to be emphasised.

The size, shapes and characteristic features of the different plant eaters and carnivores could be introduced with the models. How these different features might have helped or hindered their survival in the prehistoric world could be discussed.

The immense size and shape of certain dinosaurs could be drawn in chalk on the playground. (Older children would enjoy leading this task.)

How do we know what these creatures looked like? A reference book with pictures of fossils or reconstructed skeletons could prompt discussion.

Practical Individuals or groups could create a database of prehistoric creatures. Each database could be accompanied by a list of questions for friends to answer, for example: *Which was the biggest land creature?*

Which creatures from long ago still live on Earth today? (Crocodiles and sharks.)

What possible reasons can the children offer to explain the extinction of the dinosaurs?

Why have some prehistoric species survived? A child's hypothesis backed up with reasons based on the evidence contained in reference material should enjoy a high profile in the class discussion.

 CARE OF ANIMALS

RESOURCES *Pelican*, B. Wildsmith, Oxford University Press

Practical This popular book takes about twenty minutes to read aloud and is an excellent starting point for many of the following questions :

1. How was the pelican born?
2. Which other animals lay eggs?
3. What does an egg need in order to be safe and to produce a baby animal?
4. How do different animals protect their eggs?
5. Which skills do baby animals learn quickly from their parents?
6. What problems occur when young, wild animals are taken from their parents? When can they be returned safely to the wild?

An incubator can be loaned to the school and the interest and opportunities for firsthand observation are very exciting for young children. The care of the chicks does, however, need to be considered before launching into such a venture.

There are a number of organisations directly involved in helping to protect endangered species. For example, The World Wide Fund for Nature may be able to provide information on those creatures most at risk.

WATCH, the junior wing of the Royal Society for Nature Conservation, can be contacted at:
22, The Green
Nettleham, Lincoln LN2 2NR

LOOKING CLOSELY AT THEMSELVES

RESOURCES Mirrors (not glass)

Make available a number of mirrors, not glass, so that children can look closely at their own facial features. Ask the children to look closely at the shape of the face and then move on to the other features.

Encourage the children to describe closely the colour of their eyes. They can use primary colours to mix the right colours to match their eyes. Introduce the range of eye colours such as grey and hazel.

Set up painting or colouring equipment and materials next to the mirrors so that the children can make coloured reproductions of their face or a particular facial feature.

Make a collection of famous paintings that children can observe closely to see how famous artists have reproduced facial features.

LOOKING CLOSELY AT OTHERS

RESOURCES A photograph of each pupil

Ask the children to bring along a recent photograph of themselves. Display the photographs in a suitable position so that the children can look closely at each of the photographs on display.

Discuss with the children the different ways in which they can describe themselves and others. Children should be encouraged to look at as many features as possible including hair colour and texture, eye colour, shape of face and height. Describing others should be treated sensitively and children should be encouraged to describe only the positive features of themselves and others.

Look at the photographs and describe what they tell you about another child in the class. Look at features that are common to all the children (parts of the body). Look at features that are different (size, hair and eye colour).

Once children have developed the skills of observing and describing they can be asked to describe a photograph and see if the other children know who is being described. Which feature described made it clear who the photograph was of?

8   COLLECTING DATA

Practical   Children could gather information about their heights, arm spans, length of legs etc. and produce a series of graphs for display around the classroom.

The children could collect data about themselves and each other and start their own personal information file. A data file could be compiled on a simple database.

Using the data file children could answer questions such as; 'Who is the tallest in the class?' As an alternative everybody's height could be recorded by using life size 'cut-outs'. The children could be involved in arranging the information to show the order of height within their class or group of friends.

The information gathered can be placed on display and may prove useful when undertaking the investigation.

All of the information gathered should be aimed at developing children's awareness of the fact that we have physical differences.

INVESTIGATION   Humans as organisms

You are going to investigate the way that animals gather information about the world around them by using their senses.

Before the investigation children should have undertaken the activities listed but particularly the activity on the senses. Before beginning the investigation the children should have some knowledge about each of the senses.

This investigation has been planned as an early scientific investigation for young children to undertake. The investigation is made up of several studies aimed at developing in young children an understanding of some of the aspects of a science investigation.

Aim to develop a scientific vocabulary that children develop throughout the study and use when explaining aspects of the investigation to others.

This particular investigation is designed to be more teacher directed and led than others listed in this book. It is important at Key Stages 1 and 2 to plan simple 'investigations' to begin with to develop children's understanding. Children will need to undertake a number of investigations which increasingly place more responsibility on them for the planning, setting up, recording and drawing of conclusions aspects of the investigation.

As this investigation is more teacher directed and consists of a number of short 'investigations' it is envisaged that schools would plan for this to be the first unit of work that children undertake at Key Stage 1.

THE INVESTIGATIONS

i) Listening

This investigation is intended to be teacher led to demonstrate to the children how to undertake a simple scientific investigation.

In the classroom

Talk to the children about the two instruments you have chosen to use and look at how the sounds are made. Ask the children to explain any differences they notice about the instruments.

Provide opportunities for the children to play the instruments, showing them the correct ways and emphasising the care they should take when playing any musical instrument.

Develop an understanding of the different sounds that are made, the different ways in which the sounds are made and the volume produced (develop a working vocabulary – loud, louder, loudest).

Explain to the children that they are going to undertake a scientific investigation. Explain aspects of the investigation that you feel they should take particular care in undertaking, i.e. listening carefully and quietly to the sounds when out on the field.

Out on the field

Work with the whole class. Give one child responsibility for playing an instrument whilst the other children walk slowly across the field with their backs to the player. Ensure the child is not playing the instrument too loudly or you may have a long walk!

Keep your backs to the player, or have the player play from behind a wall or other object in order to keep the distance you walk to a minimum.

Once you cannot hear the instrument stop and place a marker on the field.

Now undertake the same investigation, in exactly the same way, with the other instrument. If the teacher feels that the children would understand then the same investigation can be repeated to check the same results are obtained. If the results prove different then a marker can be placed between the two sets of results, the average, which the children will feel is fair.

Once the investigation is complete talk through the results and record and display them in the classroom.

Resources

- two musical instruments with distinctive variation in sound and volume
- markers to indicate distances on the playing field
- measuring instruments (non-standard measures can be used with young children)

Cross-curricular links
GEOGRAPHY

A class display

The teacher could construct a simple graph, in the form of the school field, and ask the children place pictures of the musical instruments at distances across it. The distances are not important but the order in which the instruments are set out is and for some children the degree of difference between each instrument will be important.

Talk through with the whole class emphasising:

- that different instruments can be heard over greater distances;
- that different instruments make different degrees of sound (volume);
- the need to record our results so that others will understand;
- the information that their 'graph' provides for others;
- the ways in which science investigations are undertaken.

ii) Looking

Looking closely at photographs

Obtain a large colour action photograph containing lots of detail that the children can describe. Over a period of time draw up a list of all the things they can see and describe in the photograph. Short periods of time can be found when the class is sat around the teacher and can be encouraged to look closely at the photograph and add a description to those on display. Once the whole class has been encouraged to observe the photograph then individuals and pairs of children can find time to look closely themselves and provide new observations.

Later in the term new lists can be added that identify what the children can see but cannot hear, taste, smell or touch in the photograph.

Looking closely at ourselves and others

Provide opportunities for children to look closely at themselves and others and to draw or paint what they see.

Provide plastic mirrors and viewers to encourage them to look in more detail at what they can see.

Display their paintings and drawings and encourage others to evaluate them in terms of the amount of information they provide about somebody. What is it about one painting that helps you to identify who it is?

Talk through with the whole class emphasising:
- that you need to look closely to see things in detail;
- that there are things that sight alone cannot tell us;
- that our senses together can provide us with a great deal of information;
- the need to record our results so that others will understand;
- that scientists have to look closely at everyday things to understand them more.

iii) Touching

Make a 'feely' bag or wrap some everyday objects in material. Ask the children to feel the objects and explain what they think they are. Placing a blindfold on a child makes them imagine more the shape and feel of an object and can be used to emphasise the need for a fair test.

Resources
- a number of everyday objects that the children will be familiar with
- several objects that will be unfamiliar to the children and have interesting shapes, eg a garlic crusher
- a blindfold

Work with the whole class to begin with, showing them the care they should take and how they might record what they think the object is. They can simply draw the object and then make comparisons between the drawings, when children will notice that some drawings provide more detail. Discuss this with the children to encourage them to take more care over feeling and imagining the shape of the object.

Encourage children to place as much information as possible on their drawings. They may include what they think it is made of or indicate where a part is soft or round. Throughout consider ways of developing a vocabulary with which children can explain their objects to others.

Once the children are used to making detailed drawings of objects based upon their sense of touch provide them with an object that they will not be familiar with. Discuss their drawings with the whole class.

Talk through with the whole class emphasising:
- that there is information about objects that our sense of touch can provide;
- that there is information that our sense of touch cannot provide, eg colour;
- the need to record our results so that others will understand;
- the information that their drawings provides for others;
- the ways in which science investigations are undertaken.

iv) Tasting & smelling

Resources
- bags of different flavoured crisps
- a plastic cup and drinking water
- a blindfold

The two senses can be undertaken at the same time using the same resources. This provides an opportunity to make comparisons between two senses.

Place several different flavoured crisps on plates and ask the children to taste one from each plate and then say what flavour they think it is. With young children you will need to show them the crisps in their bags before you begin so that they have some idea of the flavours that you are using. With very young children just use four or five flavours – and nothing too extreme. If children show a strong dislike to the flavours then they can observe several others tasting for flavours.

Explain to the children that they should have a mouthful of water after they have tasted a crisp. Explain that this is to clean out their mouths so that they can taste clearly and that this will help them to identify the flavour.

The main observation to make is not that the children were right or wrong but that it was not easy for them to say what the flavour was each time. It may be that some crisp flavours were more easily identified than others. Why?

Undertake the smelling test in the same way. Keep the crisps in their packets to accentuate the smell and ask the children to identify the flavour when blindfolded.

Talk through with the whole class emphasising:
- that there is information about objects that our sense of smell and taste can provide;
- that there is information that our sense of touch and smell cannot provide;
- that a single sense is not always successful in helping us to identify an object;
- the ways in which science investigations are undertaken.

Note: wherever possible encourage children to:
- make predictions;
- provide information based upon what they have investigated;
- interpret charts, graphs and drawings.

Assessment

ATTAINMENT TARGET 1

Set out below are suggestions of the relevant observations you might make at levels 1 to 3 whilst the children are undertaking this investigation.

at level 1
- The children explained that the different musical instruments made different sounds and that some made loud sounds and some made even louder sounds. They could relate some of the sounds to specific instruments.
- The children have produced a painting of somebody in their class showing all the main physical features. They could explain each of the features to the teacher.
- They could explain the main features of an object placed in a feely bag. They explained in terms of the object being hard, sharp or made of metal.
- They explained that they could tell the flavour of a crisp by tasting it or by smelling it.

at level 2
- The children made suggestions as to how they might investigate which instrument could be heard from furthest away.
- The children used standard or non-standard measures to record the distance over which each sound could be heard.

■ They could describe the results of the sound investigation and have recorded the results showing clearly the distances over which each instrument could be heard.

■ They looked back at their predictions and could explain whether what they thought would happen was what did happen.

at level 3   ■ The children made simple predictions about which instruments might be heard furthest away.

■ When undertaking the sound investigation the children said that it was not a fair test because they were not hitting the instruments with the same force.

MATERIALS AND THEIR PROPERTIES

1. GROUPING MATERIALS

MATERIALS AND THEIR PROPERTIES

Work on everyday uses of materials should be related to pupils' knowledge of the properties of the materials and of objects made from them, and to their knowledge of the way changes affect the materials.

Pupils should be taught:

1. Grouping materials

a to use their senses to explore and recognise the similarities and differences between materials;

b to sort materials into groups on the basis of simple properties, including texture, appearance, transparency and whether they are magnetic or non-magnetic;

c to recognise and name common types of material, *eg metal*, *plastic*, *wood*, *paper*, *rock*, and to know that some of these materials are found naturally;

d that many materials, *eg glass*, *wood*, *wool*, have a variety of uses;

e that materials are chosen for specific uses, *eg glass for windows*, *wool for clothing*, on the basis of their properties.

SCIENCE ACTIVITIES

Before setting up the investigation, children will need to have undertaken the following activities. The activities provide the children with the opportunity to acquire the skills and knowledge they will require in order to undertake the investigation. Preparing children with the appropriate skills and knowledge will assist the teacher's organisation of the investigation.

Whilst the children are undertaking the activities the teacher should plan to develop a vocabulary with which the children can work.

ACTIVITIES

Grouping materials

SORTING MATERIALS

RESOURCES

Gather together a selection of different materials, natural and man-made, most of which children will know. Add one or two unusual materials, such as natural sponge, cork, pumice (which is a rock that floats), Plasticine and clay (in different forms). Include an example of metal, plastic, wood, paper and rock

Class discussion

Show the materials to the children asking them if they know what they are and where they came from. Explain carefully the ones that are unfamiliar to the children. Begin to develop a language for describing the different materials in terms of shape, colour, texture and use.

Practical

Children may use texture, shape, colour, transparency, whether they are magnetic or non-magnetic or where the material comes from to sort the materials. Encourage the children to think of as many adjectives as they can to describe the materials. Encourage the children to sketch and describe the materials so that they can be recognised by others. Young children enjoy seeing older children using their information in order to identify a material. Emphasis should be placed on developing the children's ability to describe different materials.

Information Technology

IT can be used here with *Branch/Sorting Game* to help the sorting. Describe the properties of the materials – try a guessing game, with children describing three properties of a material, then another child picking the material described.

NATURAL AND MANUFACTURED MATERIALS

RESOURCES

A collection of natural and manufactured materials. The collection could include such objects as seeds, wood, rocks, plastic bottle tops and bricks

Class or group discussion

Look at the materials and discuss the effect of each object upon the children's senses. Children should describe the texture, colour, hardness, size and shape of each object. Encourage them to tell you what they know about each material in terms of what it is, where it has come from, its use and how it was made. Record their observations so that they begin to form a picture of each material.

Explain to the children that some materials are natural and others are manufactured. Explain what is meant by the terms and give examples that they will be familiar with.

Practical

The children are encouraged to sort the objects into groups according to whether or not they are natural or manufactured.

Children could find out about how the manufactured items have been processed. What is the natural raw material that the manufactured examples are made from?

3 KITCHEN UTENSILS

RESOURCES | A collection of kitchen utensils

Class or group discussion

Children could be asked about why different kitchen utensils are made from different materials. Firsthand experience could be given by placing wooden spoons, and metal spoons on radiators to observe the different rates at which each material heats up. Only the teacher should undertake such an activity. Children could be introduced to the idea that some things that do *not* look hot could be. The children should be shown the correct way of testing if something is hot.

Relate the function of the different utensils with the materials they are made from.

4 INSULATING MATERIALS

RESOURCES | Fish and chips wrapped in paper

Practical | Why do fish and chip shops wrap your fish and chips in paper? Children could investigate the properties of certain materials at keeping things warm – try different papers and fabrics. Which is best? Is it the one fish and chip shops use? Children could be introduced to the idea of insulation and why it is important.

Teacher demonstration | Place some warm water in a number of containers (all the same volume, but different materials) and measure their temperature. Observe which stays warm the longest. This is an opportunity for teachers to introduce children to using a thermometer and to the planning of a fair test. Which materials kept the water warm the longest?

Where else do we use insulation? What types of materials are used for insulation?

5 EXPLORING EVERYDAY MATERIALS

RESOURCES | A collection of everyday materials – wood, stone, metal, cooking ingredients, liquids and plastics

Practical | Children examine the materials closely, describing them using their senses. They then find a range of ways in which they are used in everyday life.

The children could find real examples or find pictures of the things that make use of or are made from the materials on display.

The children should be able to say why the material is suitable for its use.

6

MIXING DRINKS

RESOURCES Selection of drinks made from cordials. (Use different flavourings and different concentrations)

Practical Ask the children to describe the taste of the drinks, and why they taste different.

Talk to the children about other substances that you can add water to. Do these substances behave in the same way? Discuss substances that disappear, those that remain the same, and those that change colour.

Investigate the following:
- equal amounts of different substances in the same volume of water;
- different water temperatures (hot, cold, luke warm) and the same amount of the same substance;
- different amounts of the same substance with the same volume of water.
Does the number of times the mixture is stirred make a difference?

This activity would be very useful to undertake before carrying out the investigation for this unit.

INVESTIGATION Materials and their Properties

"How do paper towels differ?"

Resources
- a variety of paper tissues and towels
- water
- rulers
- stop clocks
- measuring cylinders

Starting point
A collection of paper tissues and towels.

Observing and asking questions
Encourage the children to examine the collection of paper towels and tissues. The children should describe how each sample feels and what it looks like – after close observation with magnifiers. Emphasis here should be placed upon using the senses to describe the nature of the paper towels and tissues. Children should be encouraged to explain what they think the towels would be best for. For example, mopping up, drying hands or surfaces.

Children may ask
Which one of the towels is best at mopping up water spills?

Predicting
Encourage the children to make a prediction about what they think will happen and why. For example: *I think the paper towel will be best at mopping up water because we have paper towels at school for drying our hands.*

Designing and planning the investigation
The children should try to ensure that they keep the test fair by keeping everything constant apart from the paper towel or tissue they are testing.

Children could choose a minimum of three paper towels or tissues to test. Make sure the pieces of towel or tissue are all the same size. In order to make the test fair, the children will need to decide how much water will be 'mopped up', over what period of time the experiment will last and what they mean by best at 'mopping up'. Young children find it difficult to ensure that all aspects of the investigation are fair so encourage them to investigate just one variable at a time.

Decisions will need to be made by the children about how they are going to carry out their investigation and how they are going to record their findings.

The children carry out the investigation making sure that they are careful with measuring the sizes of the pieces of paper towel being used and the quantity of water to be mopped up. Consideration needs to be given to the management of this investigation to ensure the minimum of mess.

Recording

Children record their findings and explain what happened. The pieces of towel or tissue could be mounted in order of how well they 'mopped up' water. Children could record their findings as a graph. *Data Sweet* (Archimedes) could be used in this context. Emphasis should be placed on making sure that the children record and present their findings in such a way as to allow others to understand clearly what they have found out.

Drawing conclusions

Were the children's predictions correct and were they able to keep the test fair?

Some children may wish to take their investigations further.

How successful are paper towels for 'mopping up' other liquids such as vegetable oil?

Does the time given for 'mopping up' have any effect? Are some paper towels quicker than others?

Does the size of the paper towel have any effect on the speed of 'mopping up'?

The children could write to the companies who make the tissues and towels and tell them about their investigations and what they found out, requesting information about how the towels are made, and why they are made in the way they are.

Assessment

ATTAINMENT TARGET 1

Set out below are suggestions of the relevant observations you might make at levels 1 to 3 whilst the children are undertaking this investigation.

at level 1
- The children made sketches of the different materials having observed them through a hand lens.
- The children could explain the differences between the different materials using such terms as soft, rough or smooth.
- The children could explain what they did and what happened.

at level 2
- The children made simple suggestions of how they might investigate which towel would be best for mopping up water. Through further discussion with their teacher they could eventually describe how they would set about tackling the investigation.
- The children made observations about the amount of water each material soaked up.
- They compared the results for each material and could explain which was the best for mopping up water.
- They used non-standard measures to ensure that each material was placed in the same amount of water each time using a measuring container.

■ They recorded their results in graph form and could explain from their results whether the results were what they had expected.

at level 3

■ The children put forward their own ideas of how they might set about the investigation.

■ They made simple predictions such as, 'I think the paper towel will mop up the water best because we use those at school,' or 'I think this towel will be the best because it is the thickest.'

■ They used standard or non-standard measures of capacity to measure out the same amount of water for each material.

■ The children explained that each paper towel must be the same size if the test is to be fair. As the investigation proceeds the children stopped to explain that they would need to begin again as they have to allow the same amount of time for each towel to soak up the water. The children then chose to use stop clocks to record the time.

■ The results were recorded as graphs or as a display placing each material in order with the amount each soaked up set down underneath.

■ The children used their results to explain why some materials soaked up more water than others. They explained that the thicker material was best.

■ The children explained clearly to the class what they have found out and referred to their recordings throughout.

KEY STAGE 1
UNIT OF WORK
4

MATERIALS AND THEIR PROPERTIES

2. CHANGING MATERIALS

MATERIALS AND THEIR PROPERTIES

Work on everyday uses of materials should be related to pupils' knowledge of the properties of the materials and of objects made from them, and to their knowledge of the way changes affect the materials.

Pupils should be taught:

2. Changing materials

a that objects made from some materials can be changed in shape by processes including squashing, bending, twisting and stretching;

b to describe the way some everyday materials, *eg water*, *chocolate*, *bread*, *clay*, change when they are heated or cooled.

SCIENCE ACTIVITIES

Before setting up the investigation, children will need to have been provided with opportunities to handle and 'play' with a variety of different materials. Children should have experience of manipulating materials and observing and talking about changes that take place. They should observe the way that certain materials change over time. Through such experiences children should have begun to develop an understanding that some materials change by drying, cooling, manipulating or adding other substances to.

It is important to develop a vocabulary by which the children can describe the properties of different materials and the changes which they observe taking place.

ACTIVITIES — Changing materials

SOIL

RESOURCES

A collection of different soils. These can be made up quite easily by gathering a selection of differently sized gravels and sands from a builder's yard and mixing in different proportions with soil

Practical

Children should examine the soils closely (wearing disposable gloves) describing the features of the soils – texture, colour, constituent parts. What can be found in the soil? Are all the soils the same? Children could progress to investigate how the soil changes when it is wet or dry.

Children could investigate how well different soils drain – are some soils better for growing things in than others?

THE WATER TRAY

RESOURCES

The 'water tray'. This should contain a variety of objects that squirt and pour

Practical

Try pouring water with a variety of pouring devices – encourage the children to describe what they feel and see. If the children pour the water from different heights, what do they notice?

Using different types of squirters, such as syringes, washing-up liquid bottles, pumps: does the amount of pressure applied affect how the water squirts?

Try mapping the pathway of the water.

Teachers should be developing the children's understanding of the properties of water in terms that it can be poured, squeezed through tiny holes, run along certain objects, etc.

DOUGH, CLAY AND JELLY CUBES

RESOURCES

Flour, water and yeast for making dough. Mixing bowl and wooden spoon. Clay and shaping tools. Jelly cubes and bowl for melting cubes in. Large thermometer

Provide the children with opportunities to make dough, clay models and to melt jelly cubes.

The focus for the activities should be on developing an understanding of the effects of heating and cooling on certain materials.

Children should also be gaining an understanding that temperature is a measure of how hot and cold things are. With young children use a large thermometer so that they can see the change in temperature when hot water is poured over the jelly cubes. It is sufficient for young children to see the rise and fall on the thermometer, they don't need to make specific readings in centigrade.

Make sketches of the dough, clay and jelly before and after heating and make notes of the changes that have taken place.

The jelly cubes can be melted and then placed in a fridge to observe the effects of cooling.

Extension activities

Observe the same amounts of dough baked in an oven for different lengths of time. Discuss the properties such as colour, texture and size. Children can also compare the inside of the dough to the outside.

Clay models can be left to dry and measurements taken, over a period of time, of their weight.

Health warning

!

Explain to children the need for maintaining high standards of hygiene when cooking and the health factors involved in keeping our hands and cooking utensils clean.

INVESTIGATION

Changing materials

"How does heat affect wax, ice, chocolate and jelly?"

Resources
- heat source
- wax, ice cubes, chocolate blocks, jelly cubes
- suitable heat-resistant containers
- water
- a safe area in which to work
- scales
- stop clocks
- large, easy-to-read thermometers

Whenever children investigate using heat and how it affects the speed of melting, very close supervision will be needed. It should not be necessary to work with very high temperatures particularly if the children work with ice or chocolate. Warm water should be sufficient to begin the melting process.

Predicting
Discuss with the children what the chosen solids are and encourage them to describe their properties. Talk about the simple properties of solids and compare them to liquids and gases. What do the children think will happen to these solids when they are heated? Encourage them to predict what they think will happen.

Most children will be able to relate their predictions to everyday experiences of handling or observing melting ice, chocolate or jelly, and so you should expect them to give reasonably accurate explanations for their predictions.

Carrying out the investigation
Investigate with one focus at a time. Encourage the children to think carefully about how they will make their experiments fair.

Investigating different solids
Choose a variety of solids to investigate such as jelly, chocolate, ice and wax. Encourage the children to set up a fair test by ensuring that the amount of each solid is the same. They may need help in weighing equal amounts.

The only factor that should change in this investigation is the type of substance. Place the solids in water of the same temperature, and observe and time the different rates at which they melt.

Investigating different temperatures
Measuring different temperatures and keeping the test fair will provide a challenge. The investigation can involve placing the solids in bowls of cold, warm and hot water. (For safety and ease of undertaking the investigation, place the solids in small plastic bowls which can then be put in a larger bowl of water.) The type of solid used and the amount placed in each bowl must be kept constant; only the temperature should be changed.

Give the children the opportunity to choose the equipment they need to set up the investigation. They will need to make decisions about the point at which they will call their sample 'melted'. The melting of each solid needs to be timed carefully to see if there are any significant changes.

Drawing conclusions

Ask the children to decide how they will record their results so that other children can understand their findings. Encourage them to record actual data rather than just simple observations.

Provide opportunities to draw conclusions from the data and to suggest explanations. If the preliminary activities have been completed, then the children's original predictions are likely to have been well-informed. Encourage them to look for patterns in the data they have collected and to point out anything that they did not expect.

Assessment

ATTAINMENT TARGET 1

Set out below are the descriptions for levels 1 to 3, and the relevant observations you might make when the children are undertaking this investigation.

at level 1
- The children described simple features about wax, ice, chocolate, jelly or any other material used. They noted how ice is cold and will melt, or that jelly wobbles and wax is hard.
- Some children explained what happened to the jelly when they placed it in warm water.
- Other children made a series of drawings showing the ways the materials changed through heating.

at level 2
- The children explained how they found out which of the materials would melt quickly in warm water. They used the thermometers, scales or stop clocks within the course of their investigation.
- The children explained what happened when the materials melted and that they melted at different rates.
- Several children had recorded the changing rates at which the materials melted and had drawn up a table of their results. They explained that they thought the jelly would take the longest to melt but the wax took longer.

at level 3
- The children explained how they might find out which of the materials would melt quickly in warm water and made predictions of the order in which they would melt.
- They also explained how they would make the test fair. There were a variety of suggestions, including: not timing until all the water was poured over the material; not stopping the clock until all the material had melted; only stirring once and for the same length of time; making sure that the warm water was the same temperature for each material; weighing each object.
- Some children explained after the investigation what they should have done to make their tests fairer.
- Other children said the results for one solid were wrong because they stirred it when melting and they didn't do that for the other solids.
- The children gave reasons for the different melting rates. Some suggested that some materials were 'more solid than others' or 'harder' and therefore took longer; others added that the heaviest took longer to melt.
- The children kept records of what they did and of their results. They explained these to the teacher and to the rest of the class. They began to refer to their records and some children used them to explain why another child's prediction was incorrect.

KEY STAGE 1

UNIT OF WORK

5

PHYSICAL PROCESSES

1. ELECTRICITY

PHYSICAL PROCESSES

Work on observable effects should be related to pupils' knowledge of physical phenomena.

Pupils should be taught:

1. Electricity

a that many everyday appliances use electricity;

b to construct simple circuits involving batteries, wires, bulbs and buzzers;

c that electrical devices will not work if there is a break in the circuit.

ACTIVITIES

Electricity

1

ELECTRICITY IN THE HOME

RESOURCES A collection of common electrical items found in the home and at school

Class discussion Explain that each item needs electricity in order to work. Electricity is produced far away and enters our homes and schools through electrical wires and we connect our appliances to the electricity by plugging into a socket.

Ask the children to imagine how different our homes would be without electricity. Explain that electricity can be dangerous and so we need to take special care when using anything connected to electricity.

Practical Walk around school and spot the items that use electricity. Use the opportunity to explain how some of the items are used, for example, the photocopier. Explain the school rules for using anything electrical, for example, setting up the computer.

Class discussion Discuss ways in which they can ensure no accidents happen in their own homes.

Electrical circuits

RESOURCES   A collection of electrical items in shoe boxes

Organise the children to work in pairs and work with as many children as you feel confident with. Place the following items in the shoe boxes: short lengths of wire with the ends stripped and exposed wire twisted, two 1.5 V 'C' batteries, two 2.5 V round MES bulbs, a 3 V to 6 V buzzer and a 1.5 V DC motor.

Explain that batteries are a source of energy. They store energy that can be used to make things work. They only have a certain amount of energy and cannot make every electrical appliance work but they have enough energy to work the items in the box.

Practical   Describe the items in the box and ask the children to work in pairs to make the bulb light, the buzzer buzz and the motor turn.

Encourage the children to help each other. Once they have discovered how to get an item to work, then get them to explain to others how they did it. This will help to clarify whether they understand fully how to make a complete circuit or whether they managed to make an item work by accident.

Get the children to explain to others how they got each item to work. Ask the children to choose one item and to draw clearly the completed circuit.

Explain that when something works it is proof that they have made a complete circuit.

INVESTIGATION **Electricity**

There are no scientific investigations that can be undertaken using the knowledge and skills acquired through the previous activities.

Teachers are advised to develop the children's understanding of an electrical circuit further by planning a Design and Technology activity that provides an opportunity for children to incorporate a simple circuit.

The following is a list of possible Design and Technology activities that could provide an extension to work on electricity:
■ design a clown or robot and incorporate eyes that light up;
■ design and make a simple torch;
■ design a vehicle with lights.

Electricity Books 1 and 2 (see Appendix 2 Bibliography for further details) provide other ideas for simple Design and Technology activities.

KEY STAGE 1

UNIT OF WORK

6

PHYSICAL PROCESSES

2. FORCES AND MOTION

PHYSICAL PROCESSES

Work on observable effects should be related to pupils' knowledge of physical phenomena.

Pupils should be taught:

2. Forces and motion

a to describe the movement of familiar things, *eg cars getting faster, slowing down, changing direction*;

b that both pushes and pulls are examples of forces;

c that forces can make things speed up, slow down or change direction;

d that forces can change the shapes of objects.

In order to develop an understanding of forces young children need to be given a wide range of activities throughout Key Stage 1.

SCIENCE ACTIVITIES

Before setting up the investigation, children will need to have undertaken the following activities. The activities provide the children with the opportunity to acquire the skills and knowledge they will require in order to undertake the investigation. Preparing children with the appropriate skills and knowledge will assist the teacher's organisation of the investigation.

Whilst the children are undertaking the activities the teacher should plan to develop a vocabulary with which the children can work.

ACTIVITIES

Forces and motion

THE WATER TRAY

RESOURCES Water tray containing a variety of objects

Practical Children should have opportunities to work at the water trays. They should develop an understanding that some objects sink, some float and others are suspended in water. Children should understand that mass and shape can affect whether an object floats or sinks.

Place a number of objects in a water tray. Ensure that some objects float, some sink and others are suspended. Let the children play at the water tray to develop an understanding. They should notice that the shape of an object can affect whether or not it floats. Provide objects that can both float and sink, such as a metal plate. Show the children that there are ways in which some objects can be made to both float and sink.

2 TOYS

RESOURCES | A collection of toys

Collect some toys that can be pushed along. Provide a ramp for the children to observe how the toys travel down it. Which toys travel the fastest, straightest or slowest? Can the children think of any reasons for their observations?

Push some toy cars along a flat surface. How can you ensure that you apply the same force to each vehicle? Which cars travel the furthest and the shortest distances?

3 CHANGING SHAPES

RESOURCES | Clay, Plasticine, soft balls

Ask the children to work with clay or Plasticine to make a variety of different shapes. Help them to understand that they are applying a force to the material in order to change its shape.

Find a soft ball and then ask the children to consider what happens to the shape of the ball when it is struck by a hand or a foot.

Developing a scientific vocabulary

Through practical activities and group and class discussion aim to develop a scientific vocabulary. Encourage children to describe the movement of vehicles and toys in terms of them getting faster, slowing down and changing direction.

Aim for children to be able to explain that pushes and pulls are forces that can act upon a body to make it slow down, speed up or change direction.

When working with pliable materials such as clay or Plasticine discuss with the children how the forces act upon the materials to change their shape.

Cross-curricular links PHYSICAL EDUCATION

Offers many opportunities for children to be involved in pushing and pulling activities. Specific lessons could be planned to develop a greater understanding that pushes and pulls can make things move, speed up, slow down, or stop. Children should understand that forces affect the position, movement and shape of an object, and that a force is required to move an object and the greater the force the greater the movement.

Dance and work with small apparatus offer most opportunities to develop an understanding of forces.

Develop an understanding that different objects that float do so at different levels. Children should be given the opportunity to relate their experiences to water safety.

INVESTIGATION Forces and motion

Resources
- Plasticine, fabrics, sheets of paper, tissue paper
- scissors, measuring tapes and rulers, stop clocks
- balls, feathers, small stones

Starting points
Begin with a recap by asking the children to describe the changes that they have observed so far.

Discuss the ways in which different objects fall to the ground. Have the children ever seen a parachute descent? Demonstrate the process by attaching the handles of a small bag containing a light weight to the four corners of a handkerchief.

Discuss the various objects that are going to be used in the investigations, and ask the children to explain the similarities and differences between them.

Observing and asking questions
Ask the children to consider how each object will fall to the ground when dropped. Will they all fall in the same way?

Which objects do the children think will fall to the ground first and which ones last? Can they give reasons for their predictions?

Try to provide an area where children can drop the objects from a height, or they will not notice any significant difference in the rate of fall. As timing may be difficult due to the speed of the descent, the children can simply observe those that fall quickly and those that fall slowly.

Investigation 1
Select a number of objects that will obviously fall to the ground at different rates such as a feather, a small stone and some fabric. Ask the children to place these objects in the order in which they predict they will fall to the ground. How can they check if their predicted order is right?

Investigation 2
Choose a material that the children can cut and shape. Ask them to consider how they can change its shape so that it falls quickly or slowly to the ground. Paper or tissue paper is the most versatile. When asked to explain how they will ensure that the test is fair, the children may suggest that the material needs to be dropped from the same height, or that they use the same amount of material each time.

Ask them to think of a few different shapes and make predictions before they begin the practical work. How can they compare the speed at which each shape falls?

Recording
Pictograms, block and line graphs, or sets could be used to record the data. The objects can be set out on a 3D display alongside the children's recordings.

Drawing conclusions
Give the children the opportunity to talk about their investigations. They can look at their original predictions to see if they were accurate. It will also be interesting to hear what explanations the children give for the data they have obtained.

Assessment

ATTAINMENT TARGET 1

Set out below are suggestions of the relevant observations you might make at levels 1 to 3 whilst the children are undertaking this investigation.

at level 1
- The children identified differences between the objects used in the investigation, that some were heavier and that others fell faster through the air. They explained these differences to the teacher or other children.
- They noted that some objects fell down more quickly than others.
- They explained to the teacher what they did and what they found out.
- Some children made a chart showing the objects they used and the time that each one took to fall to the ground.

at level 2
- The children responded to questions such as 'How might we find out which of these objects will fall to the floor first?' They suggested ways in which they could find out and, with help from the teacher, managed to plan their investigation.
- Other children undertook the investigation once the teacher had explained what to do and ensured that they knew what they were going to investigate. They suggested ways in which the investigation might be changed.
- Rulers or stop watches were used within the course of these investigations.
- The children explained to the teacher what they did and what happened. They had kept simple recordings of the time taken for each object to fall. The data collected was set out on a simple block graph.
- The children explained that what they predicted would happen didn't happen.

at level 3
- The children predicted which object or shape would fall most quickly and which most slowly. Some gave reasons for their predictions. One child said that the heaviest would fall the quickest.
- The children explained how the investigation could be undertaken and how they might ensure that the investigation is fair. They were not completely right and needed help from the teacher. They explained that the objects should be dropped from the same height or that the area or shape of each material used should be the same.
- When the children were undertaking the test, some said that they needed to start again or change the way they were undertaking the test as it was not a fair one.
- Records were kept and the children explained them to the teacher and other children. The children gave reasons for their observations and measurements.

PHYSICAL PROCESSES

3. LIGHT AND SOUND

PHYSICAL PROCESSES

Work on observable effects should be related to pupils' knowledge of physical phenomena.

Pupils should be taught:

3. Light and sound

a that light comes from a variety of sources, including the Sun;

light and dark   **b** that darkness is the absence of light;

making and detecting sounds

c that there are many kinds of sound and many sources of sound;

d that sounds travel away from sources, getting fainter as they do so;

e that sounds are heard when they enter the ear.

SCIENCE ACTIVITIES

Before setting up the investigation, children will need to have undertaken the following activities. The activities provide the children with the opportunity to acquire the skills and knowledge they will require in order to undertake the investigation. Preparing children with the appropriate skills and knowledge will assist the teacher's organisation of the investigation.

Whilst the children are undertaking the activities the teacher should plan to develop a vocabulary with which the children can work.

ACTIVITIES   Light and sound

SHADOWS

RESOURCES   A bright light source, a white sheet or piece of card stuck onto the wall and several different shapes cut out of thick black card

Discussion and observation   Switch on the light source and place an object between the light and the wall. Ask the children what you have created.

Ask the children to explain in their own words why the shadow is created.

Teacher information   Children need to develop an understanding that an object placed in front of a light source will cast a shadow. The shadow is cast due to an absence of light.

Place different objects in front of the light source but the same distance away. Let the children observe the different shaped shadows created.

Ask the children to predict what they think will happen if you move the shape towards the light source or away from the source. Were they right?

Children can measure the size of the shadows at set distances away from the light source. Is the shadow twice as big when it is twice the distance away from the light?

! Explain to the children that they must not touch the light source once it is switched on as they might get burnt.

Extension activity
Children enjoy making shadow puppets from card and creating movement by attaching the parts of the body using paper clips. Attach several sticks to the puppet to enable the children to create movement in front of the light source. Simple puppet shows can be written and presented to the class.

2 MUSICAL INSTRUMENTS

RESOURCES
A collection of musical instruments. Explain how sound is produced from each instrument. There should be a wide range of instruments to ensure that the children are introduced to the fact that sound can be produced by plucking, striking, stroking, banging

Practical
Give the children an opportunity to use the instruments and explore the sound they make. Can they change the sounds they make? How? Can they change the volume of sound created? How?

Children should be beginning to develop the idea that sound is made when something vibrates. They may be able to observe this in stringed instruments and can certainly feel the vibration in most instruments. They should understand that in order to set up a vibration an object has to be struck in some way.

Children should be developing an understanding that volume can be controlled not only by the force with which an object is struck but by the addition of a 'box' that amplifies the sound.

Once the children are aware of the key elements involved in creating and controlling sound they can set about designing and making their own instruments in Design and Technology. They can then work in music to compose and perform their own tunes.

3 REFLECTING LIGHT AND SOUND

RESOURCES
A number of reflective plates (not glass), tubes of various lengths, card of different sizes and thicknesses, black and white card and sugar paper, Blu-Tack, Sellotape, some photographs to use as an image if required and any other useful materials you have to hand. If children require more tubes than you have, encourage them to make their own

Class or group demonstration
Demonstrate how light, an image and sound can travel in a straight line to reach our eyes or ears. Use a long tube to demonstrate sound, a torch for light and yourself for the image.

Practical   Ask the children if they can get sound, light, or an image to go in a crooked line or an arc. Can they bend light, sound or an image?

Go through the resources that are available as these may give them some idea of how to start. Discuss their plans so that they are clear about what they are going to do before they begin.

Encourage children who may come up with original ideas and only encourage them to try another method if you can see that they will have great problems leading to frustration.

Recording   The recording is more likely to be the final solution they devise and they should not be forced to write up and record everything they have done just because it is a science lesson.

Practical   Set up a display in the classroom with a series of questions which invite the children to explore:
1. The effect of shining a light on a prism. What has been created? Have they seen anything like it before?
2. A selection of materials, some of which let light pass through and some that do not. Encourage the children to combine the materials and observe the effects of shining light onto the different materials. Which materials let light shine through? Which materials reflect light? Which materials when combined stop the light waves passing through?
3. A selection of light filters and the effect of light shining through them. Which colours can they create by combining the filters?
4. The casting of shadows onto a white sheet of card. Be careful if using a lamp as children could get burnt.

Find time to talk to the whole class about what they have discovered at the display. When discussing their observations encourage them to use the correct language and to describe things in scientific terms whenever possible.

INVESTIGATION   Light and sound

"Which sounds can be heard furthest away?"

Resources
- A collection of musical instruments. Ensure that you have a wide enough range of instruments to allow the children to classify them into those that are struck, plucked or blown.

Starting points
The children should have been provided with time to investigate the different sounds made by each musical instrument.

The children should have developed an understanding that there are different ways in which sound can be made and the instruments can be classified accordingly.

Provide opportunities for the children to classify the instruments you have gathered together according to how the sound is made.

Develop an understanding that there are a variety of sounds and ways in which they are created and altered.

Observing and asking questions
Ask the children to consider how they might set up an investigation to explore which of the instruments can be heard the furthest away?

The teacher will need to ensure that the children have considered how each sound is to be created. They will also need to consider where the investigation will take place as the classroom will not provide sufficient space in which to undertake the investigation.

Teacher guidance

The investigation can be undertaken on a playground or playing field. If the children are used to undertaking investigations and are capable of working with some degree of independence, then they can work in groups once the teacher is confident that they have thought through each stage. If the children are not used to undertaking an investigation then the teacher may decide to carry out the investigation into sounds with the whole class. The teacher can lead the whole class through each stage of the investigation to provide the children with a clear structure for any future investigations that they undertake.

Ask the children to make a prediction of what they think may be the result of their recordings. Which instrument do they think will make a sound that can be heard furthest away? Ask the children to rank each of the instruments that they are going to test. Record their rankings so that they can compare their predictions with their findings.

The investigation

Explain to the children that they are going to investigate the sounds made by the instruments they have been given. It is best not to provide too many, four being sufficient. Emphasise that the children must create the sound from each instrument the same each time to ensure that they create the same sound throughout.

The children will be required to measure accurately the distance over which they could hear each of the sounds. Each child will want to take a turn in walking away from the sound and then indicating when they can no longer hear it. Explain to them that their results will not be the same as people's hearing varies.

The children should take careful recordings for each sound.

Recording

Results should be recorded in a simple graph form indicating the distance over which each instrument could be heard. Children should record their results to show the distances in rank order so that they can more easily make comparisons between their findings and their predictions.

Drawing conclusions

Children should be given opportunities to explain to others what they have found out about the differences in the level of sound created by each musical instrument.

Children's conclusions should be based upon their recordings.

Children should look back at their predictions and compare them with their findings.

**Cross curricular links
MUSIC**   There are different ways in which sounds can be made and musical instruments can be classified according to how the sound is created.

Assessment

ATTAINMENT TARGET 1

Set out below are suggestions of the relevant observations you might make at levels 1 to 3 whilst the children are undertaking this investigation.

at level 1
- The children could describe what they did and explained that the musical instruments made different sounds.
- They have kept simple recordings of the distance over which each sound could be heard. They explained which instrument made the loudest noise.
- They have made a series of drawings showing the order in which instruments made the loudest sound.

at level 2
- The children responded to the question: 'Which instrument do you think you will be able to hear furthest away?' They suggested ways in which they might set up the investigation, and with help from the teacher, managed to set up their investigation.
- Once the teacher had clarified what they were doing the children set up their investigation. They suggested that the drum should be struck from the same height each time.
- Standard or non-standard measures were used to measure the distance over which each sound could be heard.
- They described what they had found out.
- They explained whether the instruments that could be heard over the greater distances were the ones that they had predicted.

at level 3
- The children predicted that the sounds would be heard over different distances and could rank the order of each from 'heard furthest away' to 'heard nearest to us'. They predicted which instrument they thought would be heard over the greatest distance and could give a reason for their prediction. *'The instrument you strike will make a greater sound than one you pluck.'*
- The children explained how they would set up their investigation and how they might ensure that it was fair. They devised ways to ensure that each instrument was played in the same way each time.
- Trundle wheels were used to take careful measurements of the distances over which each instrument could be heard.
- In discussion with the teacher the children could explain why their test was fair. They explained that they had played the instrument from behind a screen so that the person listening for the sound could not see anybody playing it.
- The children could interpret their recordings and explain them to others. They compared each other's results and indicated that one result was so different from the others that it must be wrong. The teacher suggested that they undertake that particular part of the investigation again to clarify their findings.

Key Stage 2: Programme for Science

The science Orders for Key Stage 2 have been conveniently divided up into 12 units of work. This means that there is one unit of work for each of the 12 terms at Key Stage 2.

Each unit of work is composed of a number of activities and a scientific investigation except for unit 9 – Electricity – where it is considered that there is no appropriate scientific investigation that can be undertaken as a result of having undertaken the activities set down. Instead teachers are advised to provide opportunities for children to apply the knowledge gained from undertaking the activities for this unit within a Design and Technology project. Examples of such projects have been provided.

Together the units of work combine to ensure full coverage of the aspects of the Programme of Study identified at the start of the unit.

Each unit of work consists of a number of activities followed by an investigation. The activities have been planned to provide the knowledge, skills and experiences required to undertake the investigation for that unit of work. It is expected that the activities will always be undertaken before attempting the scientific investigation.

Schools can choose to undertake the units of work in the terms of their own choice knowing that together they have been planned to ensure coverage of all aspects of the science Orders for Key Stage 2.

To assist schools in planning when and in which term each unit of work will be taught an example Programme for Science has been set down. On the example are set down the term when each unit might be taught. Schools may find it helpful to know the criteria used when setting down the example Programme of Science.

The units of work for Key Stage 2 were mapped out across Key Stage 2 after consideration of the following criteria:
- that each year children will experience work on each of the knowledge-based sections of the Programme of Study;
- that some units of work may be considered to be more difficult for children to understand so have been included in years 5 or 6. Unit 10 covers Forces and Matter which covers scientific concepts that the older children, having covered the previous work, may well be more able to understand;
- likewise some units of work may be considered easier to understand and so be placed earlier in Key Stage 2;
- unit 9 – Electricity – has been placed at an early stage in Key Stage 2 because the knowledge gained can be applied by the children in Design and Technology projects in later years;
- unit 2 has been left until the Summer Term for the Year 6 class who may well be undertaking work from the 'My Body' project or other health-related topic. The unit can therefore be integrated into work already planned for that term.

Schools may well have their own reasons for undertaking a unit of work in any specific term and year. They may for instance decide that all classes undertaking work from the same section of the Programme of Study each term will make too great a demand on similar resources and so plan to have classes working on units from different Sections of the Programme of Study.

Other schools may feel that all classes undertaking work from the same Section of the Programme of Study allows classes to see each others work and to relate work undertaken within each year group and so gain a wider knowledge about a number of related units. This could lead to the children having gained a greater amount of knowledge and experience that can be applied when they undertake work from the same Section of the Programme of Study the following year.

Whatever decisions schools make they will be left to adapt and change each unit of work to suit the abilities and previous experiences of their own children.

Key Stage 2: The Units of Work

Unit 1	Life Processes and Living Things	1. Life processes
Unit 2	Life Processes and Living Things	2. Humans as organisms
Unit 3	Life Processes and Living Things	3. Green plants as organisms
Unit 4	Life Processes and Living Things	4. Variation and classification
Unit 5	Life Processes and Living Things	5. Living things in their environment
Unit 6	Materials and their Properties	1. Grouping and classifying materials
Unit 7	Materials and their Properties	2. Changing materials
Unit 8	Materials and their Properties	3. Separating mixtures of materials
Unit 9	Physical Processes	1. Electricity
Unit 10	Physical Processes	2. Forces and motion
Unit 11	Physical Processes	3. Light and sound
Unit 12	Physical Processes	4. The Earth and beyond

Key Stage 2: Programme for Science

	Autumn term	Spring term	Summer term
Y3	**Unit 11** **Physical Processes** 3. Light and sound	**Unit 3** **Life Processes and Living Things** 3. Green plants as organisms	**Unit 6** **Materials and their Properties** 1. Grouping and classifying materials
Y4	**Unit 9** **Physical Processes** 1. Electricity	**Unit 4** **Life Processes and Living Things** 4. Variation and classification	**Unit 7** **Materials and their Properties** 2. Changing materials
Y5	**Unit 12** **Physical Processes** 4. The Earth and beyond	**Unit 5** **Life Processes and Living Things** 5. Living things in their environment	**Unit 8** **Materials and their Properties** 3. Separating mixtures of materials
Y6	**Unit 10** **Physical Processes** 2. Forces and motion	**Unit 1** **Life Processes and Living Things** 1. Life processes	**Unit 2** **Life Processes and Living Things** 2. Humans as organisms (My body or Health Education links)

LIFE PROCESSES AND LIVING THINGS

1. LIFE PROCESSES

LIFE PROCESSES AND LIVING THINGS

> Work on life processes should be related to pupils' knowledge of animals and plants in the local environment. Work on the variety of life in a habitat should be linked to the reasons for classifying living things.

Pupils should be taught:

1. Life processes

a that there are life processes, including nutrition, movement, growth and reproduction, common to animals, including humans;

b that there are life processes, including growth, nutrition and reproduction, common to plants.

SCIENCE ACTIVITIES

Before setting up the investigation, children will need to have undertaken the following activities. The activities provide the children with the opportunity to acquire the skills and knowledge they will require in order to undertake the investigation. Preparing children with the appropriate skills and knowledge will assist the teacher's organisation of the investigation.

Whilst the children are undertaking the activities the teacher should plan to develop a vocabulary with which the children can work.

ACTIVITIES

Life processes

LIFE PROCESSES – ANIMALS

Life cycles are best undertaken as part of a project on 'Our Bodies' or 'Health'.

It should be emphasised to children that the life processes are common to all animals and not just humans.

Nutrition   Children should develop an understanding that animals have different mouth parts for feeding on different foods. That digestion is the process of breaking food down into molecules that can be absorbed through the stomach wall. The healthy parts of the food can be transported by the blood along vessels to where it is needed.

Movement   Children should develop an understanding that animals are supported by skeletons. For some animals these skeletons are on the inside and for others on the outside.

Growth and reproduction   If you decide to discuss human reproduction with your class then ensure that you follow the school's policy on sex education.

2   LIFE PROCESSES – PLANTS

Children should gain an understanding that plants have life processes.

Nutrition   Children should develop an understanding that plants produce their own food through photosynthesis. The food can be transported along vessels to where it is needed.

Movement   Plants are supported to allow themselves to stand upright. Water in the plant helps to keep them rigid. Deprive a plant of water and watch it begin to lose its rigidity.

Growth and reproduction   See activity 3 for further details.

3   REPRODUCTION IN PLANTS

Practical   Examine the parts of a tomato plant.

Recap on work covered at Key Stage 1 on the main parts of a flowering plant. Identify these parts on the tomato plant. Discuss the function of each part explaining clearly the role of pollen in reproduction. Use a small, soft paintbrush to collect some of the pollen and place it into the flower of another tomato plant. Explain clearly the role of the wind and of other animals in the pollination of plants.

Make detailed observational drawings of the tomato plants and keep a record of each stage. Clearly show how the petals drop and how the tomato grows.

Once a large enough tomato has grown it can be cut in half to reveal the seeds growing inside. The children can make observational drawings of the cross-section of the tomato to complete their pictorial record.

INVESTIGATION   Life processes

"What do plants need to stay alive and healthy?"

Starting point
Look at a selection of different types of plants, some healthy and some unhealthy.

Observing and asking questions
Describe the plants and the differences between them. Discuss with the children:
1. What do plants need to keep healthy?
2. Why do you think some of the plants are looking unhealthy?
3. Why do plants need light, water and food?
The needs of plants could be researched.

Children may ask
Does the volume of water given to a plant affect its growth?
Does the direction of light affect how well a plant grows?
Does the quantity of soil a plant is grown in affect its growth and its health?

Resources

- variety of seedlings and plants to observe
- bean and pea seeds
- growth media: soil, compost
- plant pots
- seed trays
- rulers
- measuring cylinders
- scales

More able children may wish to investigate two things, for example, does (i) the type of water or, (ii) the quantity of water, have most effect on how healthy a plant remains?

If this investigation is carried out the child needs to perform two tests, one for each type of water and the other for quantity of water. The child should then draw conclusions based on the results of both tests.

Predicting

Before carrying out an investigation always encourage the children to make a reasoned prediction. Children working at level 5 in Sc1 should be volunteering scientific reasons for their predictions. This will mean that they require background knowledge on what plants need to stay alive and healthy.

The children may predict the following:

The seedling that we are giving most water to each week will not grow so healthily because I've noticed that when our plants are over-watered at home they sometimes die.

Or at a higher level:

The seedling that we are giving the least amount of water to each week will grow most healthily because seedlings need some water but not too much to help in the process of photosynthesis.

In this example it would be necessary to talk to the child about what they understood by photosynthesis and what was taking place in the plant for this to occur.

Designing and planning the investigation

When the children have decided what to investigate, encourage them to decide which variables they will change and which they will keep constant.

Water volume   Children investigate a minimum of three different volumes of water. The type of plant, the composition and quantity of soil, light and temperature should be kept constant. The children should be encouraged to test different volumes of water on more than one plant (five plants for each volume of water). Ensure that the volumes selected by the child are varied enough to give different results.

Light direction   A plant should be exposed to light from above, from below or from all sides. Children should investigate a minimum of three directions. All other factors in the investigation should be kept constant.

Mass of soil   Ensure that the children use the same soil composition within their investigation. They should use a minimum of three different soil masses. The same type of plant should be grown.

Small pea or bean seedlings should be used. They can be grown quickly and in large quantities for the purposes of the investigation.

Children should decide what equipment they need before beginning their investigation. They should also consider where the investigations should be sited in the classroom to avoid interference or damage.

Children should select and use appropriate measuring devices. The children need to decide what observations and measurements should be made, and how often. A suitable method of presenting their results should also be planned. At Key Stage 2 the children should be working more independently in the design and implementation of their investigations. Their tests should be fair within the restrictions of a primary classroom.

Recording

The children should record their observations clearly. Efforts should be made in Key Stage 2 to encourage the children to quantify their observations using standard measurements.

Presentation of results in tabular or graphical form should be encouraged. Children should use IT whenever possible as a means of recording and presenting their findings.

A diary may be useful in which the children could draw the plants and record observations as their investigations progress. Consideration needs to be given as to how the findings will be presented to the other children in class.

Concluding

Children examine their results and report what happened and explain why. The children should be able to say whether or not the investigation they carried out was fair. If it was not, can they explain why?

If possible the children's findings should refer to the data they have collected to add support to their conclusion.

Children should ask: *Was the prediction I made accurate?*

The children should evaluate their investigation and pass comment on whether it was successful and if there are things they would change if they were to do it a second time.

A common fault in preparing for this investigation is to grow too few seedlings for each variable being tested. The children should be encouraged to recognise that when investigating how well plants grow, germinate or stay healthy, it is better to use more than one seedling for each variable being changed in order to obtain more reliable results. For example, if the children are investigating how the quantity of water a seedling receives each week affects its health, they should have at least five seedlings for each volume of water and then a range and average growth can be calculated.

This point is unlikely to be recognised independently by the children and should be introduced as a teaching point.

Assessment

ATTAINMENT TARGET 1

To assist teachers in undertaking assessments when children are undertaking scientific investigations the following support has been compiled. It sets out suggestions of the types of responses that teachers might observe when children are undertaking this investigation. Suggestions have been set out against levels 3 to 5 but it should be recognised that there may well be children who are working outside of these levels.

at level 3

Respond to suggestions
■ The children could explain how they might set about investigating whether the amount of water you give each plant will affect how it grows. They predicted that the plant given most water would grow more than the others.

Use equipment and make observations
■ They used a metre ruler accurately to measure the growth of each plant and measuring jugs to measure out the same volume of water for each plant each week.

Carry out a fair test
■ The children have made recordings of the height of each plant twice a week. They suggested to the teacher that the recordings should be undertaken at the same times to make the investigation even fairer.

Record
■ The children made recordings twice a week and have constructed three simple graphs showing the different growth rates of each plant.

Explain observations
■ They could explain, using their graph showing the growth rate of each plant, that the data showed that one plant grew higher than all the others. They explained that their graph showed that neither the plant with little water nor the plant with most water grew the highest.

Is it what they expected?
■ They recognised that their prediction was wrong and the plant that received the most water did not grow better than the others.

at level 4

Recognise need for a fair test
■ The children planned their investigation and explained that they were going to make a fair test by providing each plant with the same amount of water at the same times each day. When they set up the investigation they asked if all their three plants could be placed side by side in the middle of the window sill to ensure that they all received the same amount of light.

Make predictions
■ The children predicted that the seeds that received the most water would die because they overwatered a plant at home and that died.

Select apparatus
■ The children decided to use a tape measure as it was easier to measure the heights of the plants than with a metre ruler.
■ They maintained accurate records throughout the period of observation.

Recording
■ The children produced three graphs showing the growth rates of each plant over a period of a few weeks.

Interpreting data

■ The children used their graphs to explain to all the class the different rates at which each plant grew. They explained that the graphs indicated that all three plants seemed to 'shrink' at one stage. They explained that this was due to the fact that when they went on their residential trip they forgot to ask anybody to water the plants and when they returned all three had begun to droop.

Drawing conclusions

■ The children explained clearly to the class that one plant grew better than all the rest. They said that they felt that this was due to the fact that plants must require just the right amount of water for growth. They explained that the plants would need water and light and nutrients to maintain growth. They recognised that when the plants went without water they all drooped so water formed part of the rigid framework of the plant that allowed it to remain upright.

at level 5

Identifying key factors

■ The children explained at the planning stage that they had to consider the amount of water, light and nutrients each plant received. They knew how to keep the light and nutrients constant for each so that they could just focus on observing the effects of water on plant growth.

Make predictions based upon scientific knowledge

■ The children predicted that the plants would require just the right amount of water to grow healthily because each would sprout, grow in height, flower and then develop seeds and at each stage it would require different amounts of water. Another child pointed out that the plants required light in order to grow and if it were sunny then it would provide better conditions for growth. This, they explained, meant that the plants would require more water on sunny days than dull days.

Select apparatus and use with precision

■ The children selected appropriate apparatus for measuring the height of each plant, volume of water to be used and weight of each plant.

Make observations or measurements

■ The children measured the growth in height of each plant with accuracy.

Repeat and explain differences they encounter

■ Another group of children had undertaken exactly the same investigation but their plants had not grown at anywhere near the same rate. This group had placed their plants in a different location and the children could explain that the different rates of growth were due to the absence of light which is required for plants to grow healthily.

Recording

■ They constructed one graph with three line graphs showing the growth rate for each plant. They explained that they had placed the growth rates for all plants onto one graph so that it would be easier to make comparisons and see the difference in rates of growth.

Drawing conclusions

■ They used the data they had collected to explain clearly that the prediction they made was correct and that you can provide plants with too little or too much water and they require just the right amount to combine with light and nutrients to ensure that a healthy plant grows.

LIFE PROCESSES AND LIVING THINGS

2. HUMANS AS ORGANISMS

LIFE PROCESSES AND LIVING THINGS

Work on life processes should be related to pupils' knowledge of animals and plants in the local environment. Work on the variety of life in a habitat should be linked to the reasons for classifying living things.

Pupils should be taught:

2. Humans as organisms

nutrition

a the functions of teeth and the importance of dental care;

b that food is needed for activity and for growth, and that an adequate and varied diet is needed to keep healthy;

circulation

c a simple model of the structure of the heart and how it acts as a pump;

d how blood circulates in the body through arteries and veins;

e the effect of exercise and rest on pulse rate;

movement

f that humans have skeletons and muscles to support their bodies and to help them to move;

growth and reproduction

g the main stages of the human life cycle;

health

h that tobacco, alcohol and other drugs can have harmful effects.

SCIENCE ACTIVITIES

Before setting up the investigation, children will need to have undertaken the following activities. The activities provide the children with the opportunity to acquire the skills and knowledge they will require in order to undertake the investigation. Preparing children with the appropriate skills and knowledge will assist the teacher's organisation of the investigation.

Whilst the children are undertaking the activities the teacher should plan to develop a vocabulary with which the children can work.

ACTIVITIES

Humans as organisms

1

THE EFFECTS OF EXERCISE ON THE BODY

Class or group discussion

Discuss how the body reacts to exercise after a physical education lesson. Children could discuss why they feel their heart beats faster when they do exercise. They could look for bodily changes during exercise, for example, breathing rate, skin colour, sweating and heart beat rate. Research work could be done to find out what is happening in this situation.

Practical

Children could investigate the differences between each other's heart beat rate and breathing rate after exercise. They could investigate different types of exercise and find out which is the most strenuous.

2

THE MAJOR ORGANS

RESOURCES

A model of the human body

Research task

Find out about the major organs of the body. Where are they situated and what are their functions? How can we keep them healthy? Knowledge of the major organs needs to be developed with children at Key Stage 2 into a fuller understanding of how the organs work within systems in the body. For example, the circulatory, digestive and nervous systems. Local hospitals and healthcare centres could be contacted for information.

Opportunities should be provided for the children to compare organ systems in humans and mammals, and to identify any similarities and differences. The local vet may be able to help with information or visit the school to answer children's questions.

3

THE HUMAN HEART

RESOURCES

A model of the heart

Class discussion

Discuss what the heart does. Research how the heart works within the whole circulatory system. Refer to arteries and veins.

Children could find out about the importance of exercise in keeping the heart working effectively. Contact the British Heart Foundation for information and details.

Practical

Children could investigate the effects of exercise on heart beat rate.

4

OUR TEETH

RESOURCES

A visit from the school dentist. Collect information relating to the job of the dentist

Class discussion

Children could find out about the nature of teeth. Why they are different shapes and what their different functions are.

How should teeth be looked after and why is it so important to do so? What things can cause decay and damage to gums and teeth?

Practical Put together a dental care advertising campaign that informs people of the importance of careful dental hygiene.

5 DISEASE

Class discussion Discuss diseases, how they are spread and how we become infected.

Practical Children should research harmful germs: viruses and bacteria.

What common diseases are caused by these agents? Children could also research into diseases that can be caught only in foreign countries.

Children find out how the body combats disease. Contact local doctors, healthcare centres and hospitals for information on how our bodies are helped to fight disease. Mention inoculation and the use of vaccines.

6 AN ANTI-SMOKING CAMPAIGN

Class discussion A discussion should be held between teachers and children on the issues against smoking.

Practical The children could research tobacco smoking and its harmful effects and why people smoke. Questions to be answered could include:
1. Where does it come from?
2. What effects does smoking have on the body?
3. Who does smoking harm most of all?
Children could contact the local health authority for information and carry out surveys to obtain people's opinions. Fact sheets and brochures could be put together to dissuade people from smoking, and placed in a doctor's surgery.

Information gained could be used to inform a debate in class over whether or not smoking should be allowed in public places.

7 HARMFUL DRUGS

This activity could follow on from the anti-smoking campaign.

Class discussion The teacher should develop the children's understanding of what drugs are. Children should find out what the differences are between drugs which are medicines and drugs which are not, through discussion.

Which drugs are illegal to use, buy and sell?

Useful publications to help teachers handle this very sensitive area of the Programme of Study include:
The Good Health Project, T. Williams, N. Welton and A. Moon, Forbes Publications
My Body Health Authority Project, Heinemann Educational
Health for Life 2, Health Education Authority's Primary School Project, Nelson.

8   X-RAYS

RESOURCES

A collection of X-ray photographs

Practical

What can the children see on the X-ray photographs? The children could be encouraged to use a picture or model of a skeleton to see if they can name the various bones. Explanation could be given as to what purposes the bones of the skeleton serve. Children could find out about the joints of the body and identify where hinge, ball and socket, and universal joints are found.

The emphasis of this activity is to develop a child's understanding of the function of the skeleton and joints in producing movement in the human body.

The children could then investigate what helps the joints to move – the use of muscles – identifying pairs of muscles that work together.

9   HEALTHY FOODS

RESOURCES

A selection of natural and processed foods

Practical

Children should group the foods into animal products and those that are grown.

Using food labels the children could investigate which of the foods have substances added to them.

Using reference material children could help to identify constituent parts of foods, as for example, protein, fat and carbohydrate – and answer questions such as:
1. What jobs do they do in the body?
2. Which foods do people think are good for them? (Give reasons.)
3. Which foods should be eaten less frequently? Why?
4. What is meant by a balanced diet?

10   RECORDING OUR GROWTH

RESOURCES

Draw up an information sheet for each child to complete

The information sheet should contain information about each child's height, leg length etc. The information sheets could also contain a photograph of each child.

A class book could be produced with information about each child. Children who join the class later in the year will need to complete a page in order that they can be involved in the work undertaken at the end of the year.

An alternative is for each child to produce their own booklet at the beginning of the year. The booklet could contain all the same information about themselves plus information about their work. Children could be asked to place one example of their best handwriting and a story that they can look back on at the end of the year to see how they have changed their style of handwriting and story writing.

At the end of the year another class book can be produced to the same format so that children can see how they have changed. Collect information together about how each child has changed. Have all children changed in the same way? What are the differences?

Information Technology

Use a database programme like *Junior Pinpoint* to create an information sheet for collecting information about each child. Ask each member of the class to complete their information sheet with information about themselves. Another database can be created at the end of the year. The children can be encouraged to ask questions about the two sets of information that leads them to search the database for the answers. For example children may ask if the tallest child in the class at the start of the year is still the tallest at the end of the year. Are boys and girls similar in height? Have boys or girls grown the most during the year?

LIFE CYCLES

Start Ask the children to bring along to school a picture of themselves when they were small.

Class discussion Talk with the children about the changes that their bodies have gone through since the photographs were taken. This is a good way into discussing the human life cycle with reference to growth and reproduction.

If you decide to explain aspects of human reproduction with your class then ensure that you are applying the school's policy on sex education.

INVESTIGATION **Exercise and rest**

Starting point
During a particularly strenuous PE lesson ask the children to describe the effects of the exercises upon their bodies. Whilst they are resting (recovering) from the exercise explain how to take each other's pulse rate. Explain that we do not need to count for a whole minute but for 15 seconds and then multiply the results by 4 to save time. Children will need practice in taking each other's pulse before they can undertake this investigation.

Observing and asking questions
Provide opportunities for the children to take and record each other's pulse rate. Collect the results together and then ask the children to look at the results and say if they feel that there are some results that cannot possibly be correct. They will notice that some results are so different from the other results that they cannot possibly be correct. This is a good exercise in teaching the children to look at patterns of numbers and in providing explanations for why some numbers don't fit the pattern. Where the figures are thought to be incorrect ask the children to try again. The children will be developing an understanding of the range of their pulse rate during lessons.

Questions you may ask
Are all children's pulse rates the same when they are doing exactly the same exercise?
Are tall people's pulse rates faster or slower than small people?
Are young children's pulse rates different from older children's?
Is an adult's pulse rate very different from a child's?

Predicting

Children will be able to make predictions about all these questions and many will provide reasons for their predictions. Before the children undertake an investigation, encourage them to record their prediction and give a reason for their prediction if they have one. Children may say that young children's pulse rates will be slower because they have less blood to move around the body. Other children may say that older children have more blood to pump around the body and the body is taller so the heart has to work harder. Children should be encouraged to relate their investigation to work they have undertaken on the heart and the circulatory system.

Planning the investigation

Children will need to gather together the correct equipment for timing and for undertaking any exercise that they may have planned. Each group should be reminded that they should not waste too much of people's time so they should ensure that they have thought the investigation out beforehand. They should, for instance, not need to wait for a whole minute when taking somebody's pulse.

Children should consider how they might make their investigation fair so that they are sure that the results they obtain from one child or group of children have been obtained under the same conditions.

Investigating age

This group can choose to select six children from the reception class and six from their own class to investigate the difference in pulse rates. Each reading will need to be taken for exactly 15 seconds to ensure the results are fair. All the children should have rested for several minutes to ensure that none have a high pulse reading because they have just been involved in strenuous exercise.

Investigating height

Choose the six tallest and six shortest children in the class and take the pulse rate of each.

Investigating the effect of exercise on the pulse rate

The children will need to design one simple exercise that all their group can undertake easily for 30 seconds. They must ensure the exercise is not too physically demanding or some children will not keep exercising for the allotted time and the investigation will not have been fair.

Some children may suggest that all the group should rest for a few minutes before they exercise so that they know that their hearts are not beating quickly before they begin the exercise.

Recording

It may be easier to devise one way of recording the results so that comparisons can be made between graphs produced for each investigation. Make the scale on each axis the same for each investigation.

Drawing conclusions

Ask each group to talk to the rest of the class and explain what they were investigating and how they set up and carried out the investigation. Ensure that the children explain their results based upon their graphs and not on what they thought would happen. Can the children give any reasons for their results? Were the results the same as they expected? Can anybody see any results that do not fit a pattern and may need to be checked?

Ask the children to look back at their predictions and any reasons they may have given for their prediction. Do their results support their prediction or not?

Make a display of the children's work and encourage them to interpret the data recorded. They may well discover other links between pulse rates and age that nobody had originally thought of.

Assessment

ATTAINMENT TARGET 1

To assist teachers in undertaking assessments when children are undertaking scientific investigations the following support has been compiled. It sets out suggestions of the types of responses that teachers might observe when children are undertaking this investigation. Suggestions have been set out against levels 3 to 5 but it should be recognised that there may well be children who are working outside of these levels.

at level 3

Respond to suggestions
- They were asked how they might investigate whether the heartbeats of younger and older children were the same after undertaking the same exercise. They could explain how they would set about the investigation and predicted that all the pulses would be almost the same after each exercise.

Use equipment and make observations
- They used a timer accurately to time the number of heartbeats in 15 seconds.
- As they began to take the first few recordings they noted that there seemed to be some difference between the rate at which different children's hearts beat after each exercise.

Carry out a fair test
- At the end of the investigation they could respond to the question, 'Was it a fair test?' They explained that they had made each child sit perfectly still for 3 minutes before he or she undertook the exercise.

Record
- They have constructed two block graphs showing the heartbeats after exercise for each child.

Explain observations
- They could explain their findings from the information on each graph. They could see the patterns and identify that one graph was different from all the rest. They suggested that this may be because they had not taken the recording correctly. They went back and checked.

Is it what they expected?
- They could see from the data that they had collected that there was a difference between the rate at which different children's hearts beat.

at level 4

Recognise need for a fair test
- They were observed explaining clearly each activity that the children were to undertake. They stopped one child because he was skipping up onto a step when all the others had stepped up. When questioned by the teacher they explained that each exercise had to be carried out in the same way otherwise it wouldn't be a fair test.

Make predictions
- They predicted that the taller children's hearts would beat faster because the body has to work harder to lift their weight.

Select apparatus
- They selected timers and recording material for the task. They could use the timers accurately.

Recording
- The children constructed one graph which combined the heartbeats of each child at rest and after exercise.
- They recorded the data using a simple database which they used to print out a graph of their results.

Interpreting data
- They used their graphs to explain how different rates had resulted from children undertaking the same exercise.

Drawing conclusions
- The children explained that their data indicated that children have different heart rates at rest and after exercise. They made other suggestions, not necessarily scientifically true, based upon the data they collected.

at level 5 ### Identifying key factors
- The children identified that they had to control the exercises in exactly the same way and repeat them for the same number of times. They explained that all the children should have a period of rest before starting each exercise.

Make predictions based upon scientific knowledge
- They predicted that the taller children's hearts would beat faster because the body has to work harder to pump the blood around a larger body and to a greater height.

Select apparatus and use with precision
- They selected appropriate timers and recording material and used them with accuracy.

Make observations or measurements
- Heartbeats were taken and recorded with accuracy. Whilst undertaking the investigation they made one child repeat the exercise because they noticed from their data that the number of heartbeats recorded could not possibly have been correct.

Repeat and explain differences they encounter
- The following week they carried out the same test with the same group of children. They noticed that several recordings were very different and explained that this could be because the children had eaten different food, had less sleep or some other reason that explained why the children's bodies were different this week from last week.

Recording
- The children constructed one graph which combined the heartbeats of each child at rest and after exercise. They have indicated the average heartbeat for their group at rest and after exercise.
- They recorded their results using a simple database and printed out their results in graphical form. They changed the style of graph because they realised that their line graphs were not as appropriate as two sets of block graphs for allowing them to interpret and explain their recordings.

Drawing conclusions
- They indicated that one child's results were very different from the others. They carried out the test again for this child to check that their results were accurate.

LIFE PROCESSES AND LIVING THINGS

3. GREEN PLANTS AS ORGANISMS

LIFE PROCESSES AND LIVING THINGS

Work on life processes should be related to pupils' knowledge of animals and plants in the local environment. Work on the variety of life in a habitat should be linked to the reasons for classifying living things.

Pupils should be taught:

3. Green plants as organisms

growth and nutrition

a that plant growth is affected by the availability of light and water, and by temperature;

b that plants need light to produce food for growth, and the importance of the leaf in this process;

c that the root anchors the plant, and that water and nutrients are taken in through the root and transported through the stem to other parts of the plant;

reproduction

d about the life cycle of flowering plants, including pollination, seed production, seed dispersal and germination.

SCIENCE ACTIVITIES

Before setting up the investigation, children will need to have undertaken the following activities. The activities provide the children with the opportunity to acquire the skills and knowledge they will require in order to undertake the investigation. Preparing children with the appropriate skills and knowledge will assist the teacher's organisation of the investigation.

Whilst the children are undertaking the activities the teacher should plan to develop a vocabulary with which the children can work.

ACTIVITIES | # Green plants as organisms

Growth and nutrition

LEAVES

| RESOURCES | A bean leaf. A selection of strong lenses |

Practical activity Children should be given opportunities to observe closely the leaf of a bean plant – or any other leaves available. They can look through strong lenses to observe closely the structure of the leaf. Bring to their attention the details of the plant and ask them to include these details in their sketches.

Direct teaching Explain to the group the function of the leaf in producing food for plant growth.

Extension activity Children can look at other leaves and note differences and similarities between the shape and structure of the leaves. They can research why leaves are different shapes and what function the shape of the leaf plays in ensuring the plant remains healthy.

ROOTS

| RESOURCES | Grow several plants. Plants with large roots are better so that children can observe the root structure more closely |

Practical activity Allow children to carefully extract a plant from the soil and dust away the soil to reveal the root structure. Bring to their attention any particular features of the root structure, eg the hairs and the fact that the roots are not green. Some children may well relate the fact that the root structure is not green to the fact that it has received no light – see activity 1.

Direct teaching Explain to the children the function of the root structure in anchoring the plant and in taking in water and nutrients.

Extension activity It may be possible, particularly on a school trip, to observe the exposed root structure of a tree and to compare it with the roots they have observed in the classroom. Explain to the children that the tree's roots have the same function as the roots of the plants that they observed.

Reproduction

THE LIFE CYCLE OF A FLOWERING PLANT

| RESOURCES | Bean plants can be used for this activity although it is advisable to use a plant with a large flower. Teachers could grow daffodils for this investigation |

Practical activity Once the daffodil has grown and flowered the children will have already gained a great deal of knowledge about the growth of plants. Now bring to their attention the flower. Explain the function of each part of the flower in ensuring that the plant produces seeds so that other daffodils will grow next year.

Explain the function of the petals and their bright colours in attracting insects to pollinate the plant. Explain that the nectar also attracts insects. Use a small paint brush to pick up some of the pollen for the children to observe. Explain the role of the wind in helping to pollinate the flowers. Observe the daffodil over time as it drops its petals and the seeds begin to grow. Make drawings to record the changes that take place in the plant.

Explain to the children how the seeds are dispersed by wind, water, birds, other animals and by simply falling around the plant. Children should be introduced to the correct terminology: pollination, seed production, seed dispersal and germination.

INVESTIGATION Light, water and temperature

A similar investigation has been written under Life processes. This investigation makes less demands upon the children to plan and organise each stage of the investigation and has been set out to be undertaken at the lower end of Key Stage 2. For this reason no suggestions have been provided for assessment at level 5.

Resources
- bean plants growing in pots
- rulers for measuring height of plants
- cupboard for growing plants in the dark
- measuring jugs for water

Starting point
Several bean plants that were planted at the same time. They should have been placed in the same sized pots in the same amount of soil.

Explaining the investigation
Once the bean plants have reached a certain height and are healthy-looking, explain to the children that they are going to investigate the effects of depriving plants of light, water or warmth so that they can observe the effects on the growth of the plants.

Before beginning the investigation the children should be clear about what they are observing and how they can ensure their investigation is fair.

Practical activity
Each group should take several bean plants and number them and make careful records of each plant before starting the investigation. The plants can be drawn, their heights measured and other details indicated such as number of leaves. The records could be kept in a book created and regularly updated by the children.

Group 1 – Light group
This group will place its bean plants in a dark cupboard. They must ensure that the plants receive water and that the cupboard is not too cold.

Group 2 – Water group
This group should keep their bean plants in the same spot where they have been growing healthily. They should ensure that their plants receive no water.

Group 3 – Temperature group
This group should place its bean plants in a cold spot where they will continue to be watered. They should ensure that the spot where the plants are placed receives sufficient light.

Group 4 – Healthy group
This group should continue to look after the remaining bean plants so that the other groups can make comparisons between their own plants and those that are remaining healthy.

Recording and reporting
Records should be taken at the same time each week by every group. Comparisons can be made about the height, colour, number of leaves and any other observations the children might make. Provide opportunities for the children to explain to others their results.

Assessment

ATTAINMENT TARGET 1

To assist teachers in undertaking assessments when children are undertaking scientific investigations the following support has been compiled. It sets out suggestions of the types of responses that teachers might observe when children are undertaking this investigation. Suggestions have been set out against levels 3 and 4 but it should be recognised that there may well be children who are working outside of these levels.

at level 3

Respond to suggestions
- They explained how they could set about investigating the effect of light on the healthy growth of a plant.
- They predicted that the plants deprived of light would not grow as long as those with light.

Use equipment and make observations
- They carefully measured the heights of the bean plants each week.

Carry out a fair test
- They ensured that each plant received the same amount of water and that the cupboard was sealed so that no light could enter through the cracks.

Record
- Measurements of height were recorded on a simple block graph.

Explain observations
- Using the graphs that they had produced the children explained the growth patterns of their plants.

Is it what they expected?
- The children explained that they had not expected the plants they placed in the cupboard to grow as long as they did.

at level 4

Recognise need for a fair test
- The children explained at the planning stage that they would need to ensure that each plant remained in the dark throughout. They also planned for the plants placed in the cupboard to receive the same amount of water as the healthy plant received.

Make predictions
- They predicted that the plant in the cupboard would not grow into a healthy plant.

Select apparatus
- Suitable apparatus was chosen by the children independently to measure the lengths of the plants and the amount of water using standard units of measure.

Recording
- The plant's growth was recorded accurately as a line graph.

Interpreting data
- They interpreted their data to explain the different rates at which the plants grew and could compare these with the graphs drawn by the healthy plant group.

Drawing conclusions
- They used their data to explain that although the plants in the dark grew taller that does not mean that they were healthy. The plants in the dark were white in colour and the healthy plants were green. They made direct comparisons between their own plants and the healthy ones placed in the light.

LIFE PROCESSES AND LIVING THINGS

4. VARIATION AND CLASSIFICATION

LIFE PROCESSES AND LIVING THINGS

Work on life processes should be related to pupils' knowledge of animals and plants in the local environment. Work on the variety of life in a habitat should be linked to the reasons for classifying living things.

Pupils should be taught:

4. Variation and classification

a how locally occurring animals and plants can be identified and assigned to groups, using keys.

Teacher information

Keys

A key is information arranged in a way that allows the children to identify an unknown species. For example, children may make a collection of twigs or leaves that they have found having visited a wooded area. They can then research the objects they have brought back into the classroom to find out as much as possible about each one. They can then devise keys by asking questions where the response is either yes or no.

There are two simple forms of keys:

A branching key:

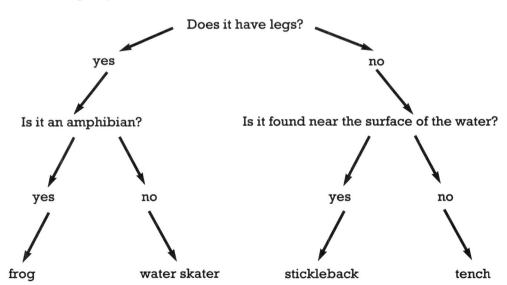

A simple yes/no key:

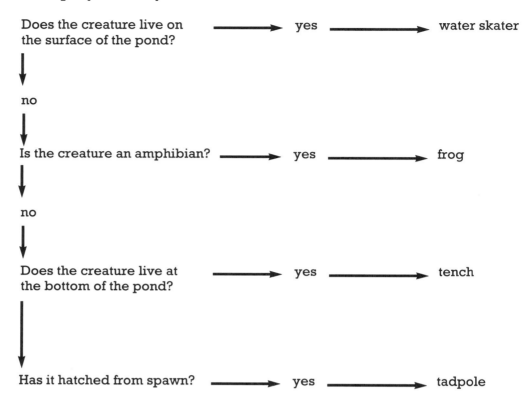

Does the creature live on the surface of the pond? ⟶ yes ⟶ water skater

no

Is the creature an amphibian? ⟶ yes ⟶ frog

no

Does the creature live at the bottom of the pond? ⟶ yes ⟶ tench

Has it hatched from spawn? ⟶ yes ⟶ tadpole

Children can devise the keys themselves or use a database on a computer.

Please note: Any project involving the use of keys is likely to be more successful if the following approach is taken:
1. Make a collection of objects for the children to observe and gather together as much information about each as possible. Encourage the children to list the information they gather about each object as this will help them to devise their own keys.
2. Explain what keys are and provide an example for the children. Simple keys can be presented and the children asked to continue them.
3. Undertake a study of a habitat where plants and animals can be studied and objects collected. This may be a local habitat, a habitat studied on a field trip or as an integral part of a geography trip.

For useful guidance on studying a habitat see: *Primary Science: A Complete Reference Guide for Key Stage 2* by Michael Evans, John Murray Publishers, ISBN 0-7195-5233-8.

SCIENCE ACTIVITIES

Before setting up the investigation, children will need to have undertaken the following activities. The activities provide the children with the opportunity to acquire the skills and knowledge they will require in order to undertake the investigation. Preparing children with the appropriate skills and knowledge will assist the teacher's organisation of the investigation.

Whilst the children are undertaking the activities the teacher should plan to develop a vocabulary with which the children can work.

ACTIVITIES

Variation and classification

USING 'BRANCH'

Branch is a simple computer program that allows children to create branching keys. It can be used on a BBC computer.

Information Technology

Branch may help the children devise questions which enable classification of observable features.

A database built up of the trees in the area could be used to teach the children the name of each tree type, and records could be made of individual tree sizes and features.

CREATING A DATABASE

RESOURCE

A suitable database for recording information about animals observed

Information Technology

If you have an Archimedes computer it is recommended that you use *Junior Pinpoint* by Longman Logotron to create and interrogate your database.

Decide whether the teacher or the children are to set up the database. This will depend upon their previous experience and the level at which they are working.

Gathering information

What type of information have you collected about the animals you are studying? How might you group the information – for example, habitat, how they move, length, colour? You may wish to decide on the headings for your database before you observe the animals to help you look for the right things.

Sorting your information

Create suitable headings for the database. For example, can the creature fly, what is its name, how long is it, what does it eat, does it prefer the dark, what colour is it, where is it found?

Interpreting your information

What questions might you ask that the database will give you information about? Print out some of the information as a graph. What do the graphs tell you about the creatures? List all the creatures that can fly. Why has the computer only found a few records to the questions you have asked?

Interrogate the database

Children could ask the computer to give information related to a number of questions that the teacher asks them. *I want to know all the creatures that fly and are longer than 15 mm.*

Can others who were not involved in drawing up your database find the answers to your questions?

CREATING AN ENVIRONMENT

RESOURCES

Woodlice or other minibeasts found in the local environment

Observation

Look under stones, bark, leaves, hedges, soil, walls etc. for a variety of creatures. Look particularly for woodlice, worms, spiders, ants, snails and beetles.

Remember to always place things back exactly how you found them. Do not destroy another creature's environment. Encourage the children to always treat creatures and their environments with care.

Do all the creatures live in the same place in the same type of environment? Look closely at their environment. What is it like? Could you re-create that environment in the classroom in order to study the creatures more closely?

Observe the creatures closely in their habitat. How do they move? What special features can you see? How do you think these creatures see, hear, smell and feel? How might we find out more about these creatures?

Take careful note of all the details that will help you re-create the right environment in which to study the creatures back in the classroom. The environment may take some time to prepare.

4 WASTE LAND

RESOURCES An area of waste land

Practical Make a study of some waste land throughout the school year. Make contact with the owner and find out as much as you can about how it has been used in the past. Has it always been waste land? Can you find evidence of what it was previously used for? Can you obtain any old photographs of the land – your local museum or paper may have photographs they may let you copy or borrow.

Decide what you might observe throughout the year or term. You could make a survey of several different areas or mark off one small section for study. How might you record how the land's appearance changes over time? Could you keep a photographic record?

Decide when you are going to study the waste land. You may decide to observe the changes at the same time of day once a month. Will what you observe vary depending upon the time of day you visit?

Study the main plants growing on the land. Do certain plants only grow in certain areas? Why? Can you find out why they only grow in these areas? How do the plants spread from one area to another?

Cross-curricular links GEOGRAPHY Can you make a map of the waste land showing all its main features and those which you have decided to observe? Make sure you identify the main physical features on your map so that others can use it to identify the location of the area you are studying. How has your map changed by the end of the year? Record these changes and discuss how the changes affect the plants and animals that live in, or use the waste area.

5 A FIELD

RESOURCES A field situated nearby that can easily be observed over a period of time

Practical Make a study of the field throughout the school year. Make contact with the owner and find out as much as you can about how it has been used in the past. Has it always been used in the same way, for example to grow crops or for grazing?

Decide what you might observe throughout the year or term. How might you record how the field changes over time? Could you keep a photographic record?

Could you arrange for the farmer or owner to come and talk to the children about what happens to the field? What questions might you and the children ask your visitor?

How does the farmer prepare the field? What are the perfect conditions for the crop to be grown in the field? Could you ask for some seeds and see if you could grow the crop in the classroom? How might you record its growth? You could compare its growth with the farmer's crop. Are there any differences in the way the crops grow? What might have caused the differences?

Does the farmer harvest all of the crop? Is any of it recycled, burned or ploughed into the land? Ask the farmer for a sample of the crop that you can bury and observe how it changes over a period of time.

**Cross-curricular links
GEOGRAPHY**

If possible plan to observe two differing localities over time so that comparisons can be made.

CLASSIFYING PLANTS AND ANIMALS

RESOURCES

Make a collection of photographs, drawings and pictures of plants or animals. Ask the children to think of ways in which they might group the different plants or animals

Practical

Explain that scientists have ways in which they group different plants or animals. Explain the ways in which plants and animals might be grouped. Develop an understanding of what makes a plant a member of one of these groups.

Children should be encouraged to consider classifying plants into groups such as ferns, conifers and flowering plants.

Animals could be grouped into vertebrate groups.

Give children the opportunity to classify animals and plants by observing closely their different features and using keys.

LEAVES

RESOURCES

A variety of leaves collected by the children

Class or group discussion

The children could be asked to look closely and make sketches of the leaves in the collection. A discussion could be based around the differences that they notice between the leaves. For example, size, shape, colour, texture and structure.

The similarities and differences in vein pattern, leaf shape and the measurement of size and area of a number of leaves could prove useful for promoting skills of observation.

The leaves could be sorted into groups or sets according to identifiable features such as shape, vein structure, size and surface texture.

From what type of tree do each of the different leaves come? The use of reference material to identify the names of local tree species and the knowledge held by the children should be encouraged.

INVESTIGATION Variation and classification

"What conditions do woodlice like to live in?"

Resources
- magnifying glasses, microscopes, hand lenses
- pooters
- observation dishes, suitable containers for holding specimens
- shoe boxes
- old fish tank
- natural material for creating habitats, eg stones, sand, leaves
- drawing, painting, sketching equipment
- camera or video camera
- tape recorder

Starting point
A walk around the school grounds, or a wild area to study minibeasts.

Observing and asking questions
The teacher needs to discuss with the children safe and careful handling of any living creatures that they find. Careful thought needs to be given as to how the woodlice that are found are going to be kept. Children need to be encouraged to use a variety of techniques for recording what they find – drawings, tables, photographs, tape and video recordings.

Ask the children to note if certain minibeasts live in similar types of conditions. Does there seem to be a pattern?

Encourage the children to look carefully at the woodlice and to describe their appearance and how they move. The children should be encouraged to sketch the areas where the minibeasts were found and to make lists or descriptions of the habitat in which they were discovered. The minibeasts can be collected using a pooter, as shown in Figure 1.

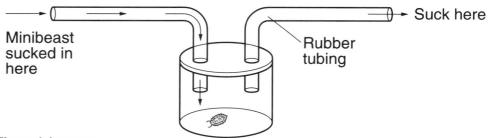

Figure 1 A pooter

Children may ask
Do woodlice choose to live where they are found because they like that type of home?
Do different woodlice prefer the same type of living conditions?
Do woodlice like the dry, damp or wet areas to live in?

What types of habitats can the children create? Make a simple list, including dry, wet, damp, light and dark.

Predicting
Before the children carry out the investigation of their choice encourage them to make a prediction about what they think is going to happen and why.

The children could use an aquarium or box in which to establish different habitats.

Children need to decide what things they are going to provide in each of the habitats. Decisions should be based upon the children's observations when they were out on the school field. Decisions also need to be made about how to set up the habitats so that the minibeasts can pass freely between the two.

How long will the minibeasts be left to make a choice and how can the children ensure that they are treated carefully?

Children need to decide how many times they will observe the woodlice, and when and how they will record their results.

Recording

Children should devise ways of recording their findings and displaying them for others to see. The results could be recorded in illustrated form along with an account of how the investigation was carried out. Emphasis should be placed on the children explaining how they ensured the safe handling of the minibeasts and how they made the investigation fair.

Wherever possible use IT to assist in the recording and presentation of work. A video camera would be an ideal means of recording and displaying to others how the minibeasts reacted to choosing a habitat.

Drawing conclusions

What did the children find out? Did the woodlice choose the environment that the children thought they would? Encourage the children wherever possible to think of reasons for what happened.

Do other animals have preferences for where they live? If so, find out about the animals' preferences and why, using reference material.

All living things should be returned, as soon as possible, to their natural environment on completion of the investigation.

Extension Activity

As a result of undertaking the investigation the children should be able to design and make the perfect luxury home for woodlice.

Assessment

ATTAINMENT TARGET 1

To assist teachers in undertaking assessments when children are undertaking scientific investigations the following support has been compiled. It sets out suggestions of the types of responses that teachers might observe when children are undertaking this investigation. Suggestions have been set out against levels 3 to 5 but it should be recognised that there may well be children who are working outside of these levels.

at level 3 **Respond to suggestions**
- The children explained how they were going to create the different habitats within their shoe box.
- They explained how they were going to undertake the investigation by observing where the woodlice were situated in their shoe box each week.

Use equipment and make observations
- They used hand lenses to observe the woodlice and made observational drawings showing some detail.

Carry out a fair test
- They explained to the teacher that they were going to observe their woodlice at the same time each day.

Record
- The children recorded on a chart where each woodlouse was observed at the same time each day.

Explain observations
- By interpreting their data the children could explain which habitat the woodlice preferred.

Is it what they expected?
- The children looked back at their prediction and explained whether what they had predicted was what had happened.

at level 4

Recognise need for a fair test
- The children decided to divide their box into four equal areas and created a different habitat in each. They explained that this made the test more fair.

Make predictions
- They predicted that the woodlice would prefer the darkest habitat because all the woodlice they found were underneath objects in dark places.

Select apparatus
- They selected hand lenses to make more detailed observations of the woodlice.

Recording
- They recorded where they had found each woodlouse at the same time each day. From their data they constructed a block graph.

Interpreting data
- The children could use their data to explain which was the most popular habitat. They also identified results that did not fit any set pattern. They explained that although one woodlouse was found on the sandy area it was probably travelling to another area when it was disturbed.

Drawing conclusions
- The children could explain the type of environment that woodlice preferred based upon the findings from their investigation.

at level 5

Identifying key factors
- The children identified at the planning stage the different key elements within each habitat. They decided that they would explore dry, damp, light and dark habitats. They explained that they had areas that were damp and dark, dry and dark, damp and light and dry and light, in order that they could clearly observe which factors were important.

Make predictions based upon scientific knowledge
- They predicted that the woodlice would prefer the damp and dark habitat because each of their woodlice was found in that type of habitat. They could also explain that their research explained the type of habitat that they preferred and they had tried to re-create the same.

Select apparatus and use with precision
- They chose to use pooters and observational containers to observe the woodlice.

Make observations or measurements
- They made detailed observations of the woodlice using appropriate magnifiers. They labelled their observational drawings and used technical terms for each part of the body having researched the information.

Repeat and explain differences they encounter
- Towards the end of the investigation they created the most popular and least popular habitats in another box to test if their findings were correct. They placed a number of woodlice in the box and recorded their movements.

Recording
- They set up a detailed plan of their aquarium and each habitat, and marked exactly where each woodlouse was observed.

Drawing conclusions
They drew conclusions about what would make a perfect habitat for woodlice. They re-created the habitat drawing upon their findings.

LIFE PROCESSES AND LIVING THINGS

5. LIVING THINGS IN THEIR ENVIRONMENT

LIFE PROCESSES AND LIVING THINGS

Work on life processes should be related to pupils' knowledge of animals and plants in the local environment. Work on the variety of life in a habitat should be linked to the reasons for classifying living things.

Pupils should be taught:

5. Living things in their environment

adaptation

a that different plants and animals are found in different habitats;

b how animals and plants in two different habitats are suited to their environment;

feeding relationships

c that food chains show feeding relationships in an ecosystem;

d that nearly all food chains start with a green plant;

micro-organisms

e that micro-organisms exist, and that many may be beneficial, *eg in the breakdown of waste*, while others may be harmful, *eg in causing disease*.

SCIENCE ACTIVITIES

Before setting up the investigation, children will need to have undertaken the following activities. The activities provide the children with the opportunity to acquire the skills and knowledge they will require in order to undertake the investigation. Preparing children with the appropriate skills and knowledge will assist the teacher's organisation of the investigation.

Whilst the children are undertaking the activities the teacher should plan to develop a vocabulary with which the children can work.

ACTIVITIES — **Adaptation**

GARDEN SNAILS

RESOURCES

A collection of garden snails

Children may be able to identify areas around school or in the neighbourhood where snails can be found.

Snails should be kept in a moist environment with a plentiful supply of fresh green plant material. Care should be encouraged if the children wish to handle the animals and a routine for ensuring the safe return of any animal to its original habitat after a short period of study should be policy throughout the school.

Practical

Sketching will help the children identify the similarities and differences between individuals in the snail collection. Colour, size, and shape could be recorded. The children may also notice other features or behavioural patterns which they would like to monitor.

Reference books will help encourage the use of correct terminology for the different parts of a snail's body, and collecting information about snails to present to friends could develop a deeper curiosity about these animals, together with a level of study appropriate to a child's interest and ability.

1. How do snails travel on different surfaces?
2. How do snails protect themselves?
3. What do snails prefer to eat?

WHERE PLANTS GROW

RESOURCES

Different plants growing in a wild area or at a site where a variety of plants growing in different locations can be observed easily

Practical

Which of the plants can the children name?

Which of the plants appear to have a variety of names offered by the children? Encourage the children to make up a name for each different plant based on observable features which can be used until reference books reveal the correct names.

Which of the plants only seem to grow well in wild areas? Which of these would be unsuitable for a garden or play area? (For example, nettles.)

The children could look carefully for clues to indicate how the different plants may be suited to their environment, for example, protection, light and moisture. Encourage the children to link their observations with their knowledge of what plants require in order to thrive.

Cross-curricular links
GEOGRAPHY

This activity can be undertaken in the local environment or on a field trip. Each child or group could choose one type of plant to study and indicate on a map where it grows best. Children should draw upon their knowledge of maps. Would somebody who did not know the area be able to find the plant you have been studying from the details given on your map?

ART

Children should be given experience of sketching and making notes at a site. Take to the study site materials for children to make detailed sketches of the plants they are studying.

ACTIVITIES Feeding relationships

1 FOOD CHAINS (1)

RESOURCES A collection of photographs that illustrate the food chain that you are going to use as an example with the children

Teacher led discussion Take a simple food chain and explain it to the children. Use your photographs to make your example clearer to the children. Your example may be as simple as:

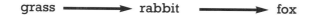

grass ⟶ rabbit ⟶ fox

Ask the children to think of their own. Ask them to explain their food chains to the rest of the class and clarify where they may have made mistakes. Praise those children who are able to design longer food chains.

Take a few of the children's food chains and place them together where everybody can see them.

Through discussion, and using the children's examples, explain to the children that:
■ food chains show a feeding relationship in an ecosystem (relate this to an ecosystem that you may have studied in the classroom or on a field trip);
■ food chains always start with a green plant.
Ask the children to check that their food chains begin with a green plant.

Information Some of the children may point out that their food chains do not begin with a green plant. Explain that the reason for this is that their food chains do not begin at the beginning but part way along the food chain. Take their examples and work them backwards to show how they always begin with a green plant.

Terminology The green plant is known as a producer. A **producer** makes complex chemicals such as **proteins** and **carbohydrates** from simple substances such as **carbon dioxide** and **water**.

A **primary** consumer feeds directly on **producers** (herbivores).

A **secondary** consumer feeds on **primary consumers** (carnivores).

2 FOOD CHAINS (2)

RESOURCES A collection of charts, drawings and reference materials on the subject of food chains

Teacher demonstration The teacher could introduce a simple food chain using animals that children will be familiar with, and develop the understanding that:
■ animals feed on one or all of: organisms, other animals and plants;
■ plants are producers, producing their own food and providing consumer's food;
■ animals are consumers, feeding on food produced by plants;
■ food chains usually begin at the producer level.

Practical Once the children are introduced to the idea of food chains, they enjoy drawing their own. The children could use reference books to compile different food chains.

Which is the longest food chain that you can research?
Which groups of animals are seldom absent in many food chains?
Explore how the children's food chains can be destroyed. Discuss the effect of taking out one member in each of the food chains.
Look for examples where food chains have been broken that children have read about in books, or that have been in the news recently.

Do all the food chains confirm the Sun as the starting point for all feeding relationships?

3 AN ECOSYSTEM

RESOURCES A visit to a wood, a pond dip or a school visit to the seaside

Before undertaking this activity children should have developed a clearer understanding of what a food chain is, and know that it always begins with a green plant.

Take the children to a pond or wood, or plan to look at an ecosystem on your next school trip. Discuss the animals and plants that they expect live in that ecosystem. They could make observational drawings of a number of plants and animals that they see.

Recap on previous work undertaken on food chains. Ask the children to draw and label the food chains that they expect exist within the ecosystem that they are observing.

Information All living things interact with each other and the habitat in which they live. This has been demonstrated in the food chains that you have already introduced the children to in the previous activities. A pond or a wood is an ecosystem. Materials are being constantly recycled within these ecosystems so that they can sustain themselves.

ACTIVITIES **Micro-organisms**

HELPFUL MICRO-ORGANISMS

Teacher explanation Explain to the children that there are micro-organisms in the air that we cannot see with our own eyes. These organisms need moisture, warmth and air in order to multiply. We can see these micro-organisms at work when we see things decay. We can control the rate at which decay occurs by not allowing the micro-organisms to multiply by ensuring they do not live in a moist, warm area with air.

cf. dry + cold conditions.

HARMFUL MICRO-ORGANISMS

Teacher explanation Work on harmful micro-organisms is best linked to a project of health or ourselves. It is important to introduce children to the fact that there are microbes that we cannot see that can be harmful to our health and bodies. The work should be extended to provide the children with guidance on how they can best protect themselves from these harmful microbes.

DECAY OF NATURAL MATERIALS

RESOURCES

A number of natural materials placed in an area of the school where they can be observed over a period of time

Class or group discussion

What is happening to these materials?

Compare the colour, shape, texture, size and weight of decaying materials with similar items in good condition.

Are there any creatures living on the decaying materials? Introduce the children to microbes and their role in the decay of materials.

Children need to be introduced to the key factors in the process of decay. These are temperature, moisture, air and microbes.

How might decay be prevented?

Practical

Place a number of natural materials outside in an area where they can be observed over a period of time. Set up a recording system so that groups of children can keep records of the effects of the elements on each object. Photographs and detailed sketches will be invaluable in recording the rate and type of decay.

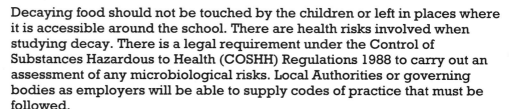

DECAY

RESOURCES

Children's lunchboxes

Practical

A collection of waste products from lunchtime could be sorted into groups. For example, wrappings, silver foil, cans, plastic containers, food.

The children should identify the different types of materials that are thrown away after any school lunchtime.

Why are these things thrown away?
What happens to them?
Are there any items which could be saved and used for another purpose?

The children need to investigate what happens to everyday waste products when they are left to decay naturally.

One collection could be buried and other items could be left to decay in the air. Comparing what happens when they are left over a period of time could include leaving some waste indoors and other materials outside.

Health and safety

Decaying food should not be touched by the children or left in places where it is accessible around the school. There are health risks involved when studying decay. There is a legal requirement under the Control of Substances Hazardous to Health (COSHH) Regulations 1988 to carry out an assessment of any microbiological risks. Local Authorities or governing bodies as employers will be able to supply codes of practice that must be followed.

Work involving decay should not be undertaken where any food will be eaten.

Only fruit and vegetables should be used and NEVER meat or products from animal sources.

Never store decaying materials in a fridge or near where food is eaten or prepared.

INVESTIGATION Decay

"How quickly do things decay?"

Resources
• two strong plastic bags with half an apple in each

Discussion
Recap with the children all the work that has previously been undertaken that relates to work on decay. They should know that some things decay and others don't and the role of micro-organisms in the decay process.

Observing and asking questions
Ask the children to look closely at the two halves of apple in the bags and to consider what might make one decay at a faster rate than the other.

Children may suggest that light, heat or moisture all have an effect on the rate of decay. Encourage the children to give reasons for their suggestions to promote such responses as:

The temperature will have an effect because we place food in the fridge to stop it from rotting.

Designing and planning the investigation
Ask the children to consider which aspect of decay they are going to investigate from the list that they have provided, eg temperature, light or moisture, and to begin to plan their investigation.

Children will need to decide exactly how they are going to ensure their investigation is a fair one by changing one factor whilst keeping other factors the same. For instance, they may need to place a small amount of water in one plastic bag and none in another and then ensure that both bags are placed where they will receive the same amount of light at the same temperature.

Health warning
Please take note of the health warning that accompanies activity 2 – Decay. Each piece of food to be observed should be placed in a strong, clear plastic bag and sealed securely. The bags should then be placed where they can be observed but not touched or moved throughout the investigation.

Predicting
Before the children undertake their investigation they should be encouraged to make a prediction. Try to encourage them to give reasons for their predictions.

Recording
The children can make simple booklets in which they record accurately the changes that take place over time by making observational drawings and sketches. The drawings may be accompanied by simple descriptions of the changes they observe taking place.

Photographs can be taken of the foods each week and kept as a record for the children to refer to.

Drawing conclusions

Children should be encouraged to look carefully at the data that they have collected when drawing conclusions.

Health warning

Please take note of the correct procedures for the disposal of the decaying foods. Do not leave on display throughout the holiday periods.

Assessment

ATTAINMENT TARGET 1

To assist teachers in undertaking assessments when children are undertaking scientific investigations the following support has been compiled. It sets out suggestions of the types of responses that teachers might observe when children are undertaking this investigation. Suggestions have been set out against levels 3 to 5 but it should be recognised that there may well be children who are working outside of these levels.

at level 3

Respond to suggestions
- The children could explain how they would set about investigating whether temperature, light or moisture affected the rate of decay.
- They predicted which piece of apple would decay most quickly.

Use equipment and make observations
- They used hand-held magnifiers to observe the decaying apples and to assist them in making their observational drawings.

Carry out a fair test
- They could explain that neither piece of apple should be moved or the test will no longer be a fair one.

Record
- The children recorded the changes by making detailed drawings each week and placing them in their booklets on Decay.

Explain observations
- The children could explain, with reference to their booklets, the changes that they had observed throughout the period of the investigation.

Is it what they expected?
- They explained that they thought it would be the other piece of apple that would decay most quickly.

at level 4

Recognise need for a fair test
- The children explained that they had placed half an apple in each of two plastic bags. They had then placed some water in one of the bags and placed the two in exactly the same position in the classroom.

Make predictions
- The children predicted that the apple with moisture in it would decay more quickly.

Select apparatus
- The children could select an appropriate free-standing magnifier to assist them in making more detailed observational drawings.

Recording
- All the children kept records in their project folders. These included sketches and written accounts.

Interpreting data

■ The children talked to the rest of the class explaining what they had found out as a result of undertaking the investigation. Their explanations were drawn from their records.

at level 5 ### Identifying key factors

■ The children explained that they had placed half an apple in each of two plastic bags. They had then placed some water in one of the bags and placed the two in exactly the same position in the classroom. When questioned they could explain that they had to place the bags in the same position so that they both received the same amount of light and heat because they were only observing the effect of moisture on the rate of decay.

Make predictions based upon scientific knowledge

■ The children predicted that the apple with moisture in it would decay more quickly because the conditions for the micro-organisms to bring about decay were better when moisture was present.

Select apparatus and use with precision

■ The children could use a maximum–minimum thermometer accurately to record the temperature ranges that their apple segments were subjected to each day.

Make observations or measurements

■ The children kept weekly records of the rate of decay of each apple piece. The observational sketches showed considerable detail.
■ They kept records of the temperature ranges recorded each day on maximum–minimum thermometers. They recorded the ranges in graphical form and drew a line to indicate the average temperature that each apple piece was subjected to during the period of the investigation.

Repeat and explain differences they encounter

■ The children set up the same investigation ensuring that the same amount of water was placed in one of the plastic bags. They then placed both pieces of apple in a dark cupboard to see if the rates of decay and their observations would be the same as when the apple pieces were placed in light.

Recording

■ The children compiled a topic booklet containing a range of methods of recording their data including graphs, observational drawings and written reports.
■ Temperature ranges were recorded accurately.

Drawing conclusions

■ The children made judgements about the effects of light, temperature and moisture on the way and rate that food decayed.
■ All their conclusions were based upon their recordings.

MATERIALS AND THEIR PROPERTIES

1. GROUPING AND CLASSIFYING MATERIALS

MATERIALS AND THEIR PROPERTIES

Work on solids, liquids and gases should be related to pupils' observations of changes that take place when materials are heated and cooled, and to ways in which mixtures can be separated.

Pupils should be taught:

1. Grouping and classifying materials

a to compare everyday materials, *eg wood*, *rock*, *iron*, *aluminium*, *paper*, *polythene*, on the basis of their properties, including hardness, strength, flexibility and magnetic behaviour, and to relate these properties to everyday uses of the materials;

b that some materials are better thermal insulators than others;

c that some materials are better electrical conductors than others;

d to describe and group rocks and soils on the basis of characteristics, including appearance, texture and permeability;

e to recognise differences between solids, liquids and gases, in terms of ease of flow and maintenance of shape and volume.

SCIENCE ACTIVITIES

Before setting up the investigation, children will need to have undertaken the following activities. The activities provide the children with the opportunity to acquire the skills and knowledge they will require in order to undertake the investigation. Preparing children with the appropriate skills and knowledge will assist the teacher's organisation of the investigation.

Whilst the children are undertaking the activities the teacher should plan to develop a vocabulary with which the children can work.

ACTIVITIES   Grouping and classifying materials

BUILDING MATERIALS

RESOURCES A collection of building materials, such as granules for cavity insulation, 'sponge' for pipe-lagging, polythene as used for damp courses, a blue-brick and roofing felt

Class or group discussion Discuss the various materials and their uses. Include some materials that may not be familiar to the children. Refer back to the work undertaken at Key Stage 1 unit of work 3 and the ways in which the children described materials and their properties.

Practical Sort the materials into groups and describe what their properties are. Why do these properties make them particularly suitable for the job they do? Children could find out if these materials have always been used for the job they now do.

If not, what was used in the past, and why is it no longer used?
What other materials might be used for the same task?

WOOD

RESOURCES A collection of different types of wood

Class or group discussion Discuss the different types of wood and where they came from. Develop the vocabulary used at Key Stage 1 for describing the properties of different materials.

Practical Many investigations can be undertaken into the properties of wood. They include flexibility and hardness. Do they all float in the same way, do different woods have different speeds of decay?

What is wood used for around the world?

Children could research into why certain types of wood are used for certain purposes. Reference should be made as to why the properties of particular types of wood make it most suitable for the job it does.

Time should be given to discuss the importance of preservation of our trees and why it is so important.

HOUSEHOLD MATERIALS

RESOURCES A collection of household materials including cooking oil, bleach, cleaning agents etc. Children should not handle harmful materials such as bleach

Class or group discussion The teacher in discussion with the children talks about what the materials are used for. Children could write 'rule books' about how and when they should be used and by whom.

The rule books should focus on where to get the information and how to use the materials, what precautions should be used and how first aid could be offered if accidents occur.

4

INSULATORS

RESOURCES

Blocks of ice cubes of the same size and stored in a thermos flask. A selection of materials for insulation. Containers of the same size and material

Practical

Discuss with the children what affects the rate at which an ice cube melts. They may suggest that it depends upon the heat, the size of the ice cube, where the ice cube is placed and whether the container is insulated.

Discuss how they might set up an investigation, using the materials set out, to investigate how long an ice cube takes to melt. Can they think of ways of ensuring the investigation is fair? They may suggest that the cubes must be the same size or that the same type of containers must be used.

The children can place the same number of ice cubes in three containers. They can place insulation around two of the containers and nothing around the third.

They can time how long it takes for each set of ice cubes to melt.

Encourage the children to record their results so that they can explain their findings to others.

5

CONDUCTORS

RESOURCES

Electrical components from which to make simple circuits. A selection of materials that are conductors and non-conductors of electricity

Practical

Ask the children to make a simple electrical circuit containing a bulb. Cut one of the wires in two and strip the ends of the wires. Place the circuit onto a board using Blu-Tack. Encourage the children to place different materials between the bare wires to see whether they allow the electrical current to flow through them to light the bulb. The children can classify the materials into conductors and non-conductors.

The same activity can be set up as a display in the classroom. Make a large circuit that can be displayed on the wall. Place a number of materials on display that children can place in the circuit.

Encourage children to bring along other materials to place in the circuit.

6

SOLIDS, LIQUIDS AND GASES

RESOURCES

A collection of photographs of solids, liquids and gases in everyday use, eg an ice cube, a river and a hot air balloon. Gather together a small collection of solids, liquids and gases for display in the classroom. For gases you could use a balloon filled partly with air, a pressurised canister (but children should not be encouraged to use it in the classroom), and a balloon pump which contains air that is to be pushed into the balloon

Class or group discussion

Try to establish how much the children already know about solids, liquids and gases. How many of each can they name? Can they describe differences between the three states of matter? How might they describe a gas to somebody who has no understanding of what a gas is? Try the same for solids and liquids?

In working with the class aim to develop a knowledge of a wide range of solids, liquids and gases. Children should also be developing an understanding of the differences between solids, liquids and gases.

Practical

Children can work in groups to make lists of the different solids, liquids and gases that they know of. More able children will be able to recognise that a car may be solid but does in fact contain gases and liquids. Develop this understanding to encourage the children to be more precise when listing their solids, eg instead of 'car' children may put 'steel' as one solid found in a car.

Make a classroom display of solids, liquids and gases from articles and photographs. Provide opportunities for the children to identify and classify the different solids, liquids and gases on display.

Cross-curricular links DESIGN AND TECHNOLOGY

Once children are confident in identifying and describing solids, liquids and gases they can be provided with an everyday object or a photograph of an object that they know well, eg a car, and encouraged to identify the solids, liquids and gases used to produce the article. This can be followed up by a visit to an industrial site where they can observe how solids, liquids and gases are used in the production of different products.

7 FLOW AND SHAPE

RESOURCES

A number of liquids that flow at different rates (different viscosities). These might include olive oil, water and syrup to illustrate the extremes of the rates at which liquids flow. A collection of solids, some of which can be manipulated. Your collection might include several rocks, clay (dry and wet) and Plasticine

Practical

Provide opportunities for the children to experience the different rates at which the liquids flow and the ways in which some solids can maintain their shape.

Children can rank the liquids from 'Flows easily' to 'Does not flow easily'. Solids can be classified into those whose shape can be changed and those whose shape cannot be changed by manipulation.

Once children have a clear understanding that liquids flow at different rates and some solids can maintain their shapes easier than others they will be able to add to your list by drawing upon their existing knowledge. They will have observed liquids being poured in cooking and the shapes of solids changed on building sites.

Some children may explain that many objects are made from a metal that was solid but that was melted into a liquid. This provides a good opportunity to develop the children's understanding that all metals can be melted, but that some require very high temperatures before they melt. The melted metal can then be moulded into the required shape in order to make the many objects we find in our everyday lives.

8 VOLUME OF SOLIDS AND LIQUIDS

RESOURCES

Water and Plasticine or equivalent

Cross-curricular links MATHEMATICS

In mathematics children can be provided with opportunities to explore the volume of shapes and liquids. They should be developing an understanding that though the shape of a solid or liquid may be changed its volume remains the same.

Teacher explanation Children will need to know how to measure the volume of solids and liquids before they can undertake this task.

Practical Children can make the same piece of Plasticine into four different solid shapes and measure the length, breadth and height of each shape. They can record their results, having worked out the volume of each shape, and observe that the different shapes had the same volume.

More able children can weigh four equal amounts of Plasticine, make a different shape from each and measure the volume of the shapes they have made.

For liquids measure out four equal amounts of water and place each amount in four different shaped plastic, see-through, containers. Ask the children to predict which has the greater volume. More able children will enjoy the challenge of finding a way of measuring the volume of a liquid.

9 EVAPORATION

RESOURCES Salt, sugar and warm water stored in a thermos flask. Saucers to put the solutions in

Practical The solutions can be used to explore evaporation. Place the solutions in saucers, to aid the rate of evaporation, and observe what happens over time. Children should be developing an understanding that solids that have been dissolved can be recovered by evaporation.

10 HOW MUCH CAN I DISSOLVE IN WATER?

Before undertaking this activity children should have developed an understanding that certain solids can dissolve in water.

RESOURCES Salt, sugar and warm water stored in a thermos flask. Clear containers that the salt and sugar can be mixed in. The children should be able to observe, through the container, whether the solid has dissolved or not

Class or group discussion Explain to the children that they are going to investigate how much sugar and salt can be dissolved in a set amount of warm water. Ask the children if they think that they can dissolve as much salt and sugar as they want into the water.

Ask the children how they think that they can ensure that their investigation is fair. They may suggest that the same amount of water is used and that the salt and sugar are measured accurately in set amounts into the water and that the solution is given the same number of stirs after each amount is placed into the water.

Stress to the children that they only place a small amount of each solid into the water at a time and observe if it dissolves. If it does dissolve then they may add a little more. It is always tempting for young children to tip large quantities into the water and then it is not easy to observe whether the solid has dissolved or not.

INVESTIGATION Grouping and classifying materials

"How are rocks different?"

Resources

Samples of:
- iron
- slate
- limestone
- granite
- clay
- sandstone
- strong magnets
- chalk
- pumice
- two-pence coins
- steel nails
- measuring cylinder
- water
- protective goggles
- strong plastic bags
- rock sample which is magnetic

Starting point

Children could examine and handle each of the rock samples. Each rock should be clearly labelled with its name or a number to identify it.

Observing and asking questions

The teacher could explain as simply as possible how rocks are made. Explanation could be given that some are created in the sea, some form deep below ground to be released through volcanoes and others are changed by the effects of heat and pressure. The children should realise that all these rocks have names and some are used for building homes, larger buildings or walls.

They should be encouraged to look closely at each rock and begin to identify certain features. What are their first impressions of the rocks? What colour are they? They should ask and answer questions about how each rock sample feels in terms of its texture and mass. The children should describe each rock using their senses and could even give each a name according to the features they identify.

As they examine the rocks using their senses they should be encouraged to find ways of sorting and classifying the rocks. This could be done by colour, hardness, ability to soak up water, shape, texture.

Children may ask

Are all rocks the same hardness?
Do all rocks soak up water?
Do some rocks break more easily than others?
Are the rocks magnetic?

The teacher could talk to the children and explain that scientists use certain tests to identify different rocks.

The children should be encouraged to suggest their own tests to identify rock types.

Predicting

Because the children have had plenty of opportunity to handle and examine the rocks before planning their investigations they should be able to give good reasons for their predictions. For example, their reasons for saying that sandstone will be good at absorbing water may well come from their observations of its texture and what the 'grains' in the rock look like. Children may well have come across some rocks in their everyday life and will be able to recall information from these experiences, for example, rocks they have found on the beach on holiday.

Designing and planning the investigation

The teacher and the children could together make a list of the tests that they have decided to carry out. The teacher could briefly describe each one so that the children are clear what they have to do. Encourage the children to think whether the test will be fair or not. They should be prompted to consider how to ensure that they carry out each test in the fairest way.

Children should be working as a group, setting out their own tests and carrying them out as carefully as possible. They should be ensuring the tests are fair each time and that they are recording their results as they progress.

Hardness   This investigation needs to be very carefully supervised and children should wear protective goggles. The children take a sample of rock each and investigate its hardness by scratching. The children could use their fingernails; if this does not make a mark try a two-pence coin. The children need to ensure that it is the same person testing each sample and that they apply a constant pressure as near as is possible.

Absorbency   Before carrying out this investigation the children will need to think carefully how they will judge how absorbent the rocks are. If all the water is to be absorbed they may have a very long wait – so decisions such as this need to be made before carrying out the test. Another factor involved is trying to ensure that each sample of rock to be tested is approximately the same mass so that the test is seen to be as fair as possible. The best way to carry out this investigation is to stand each sample rock in the same volume of water in a tray for an equal time period and then to remove the rock. The volume of water left in the tray can then be measured. The children may decide to weigh the rock before immersing it in water and then re-weigh it after a selected time period. Both approaches are equally valid providing the children give the samples long enough to absorb some water.

Brittleness   This investigation needs to be carefully supervised and the children should be wearing protective goggles. The children can take a sample of rock in a strong plastic bag and drop the bag onto a hard surface, or have masses dropped onto it. (Do not use hammers to break the rocks.)

The children need to ensure that the rock samples or masses are dropped from the same height in order to make the test fair. The children could use part of a carpet roll middle to enclose the rocks to prevent pieces of shattered rock from being scattered. If none of the rocks break then the children should increase either the height from which the rocks are dropped or the mass which is being dropped on them.

Magnetism   The children could use a strong magnet placed next to the rock to see if they can feel any attraction.

Recording
The children should record their results clearly so that they can explain what they have done and can compare their results. They should be asked why they think they got the results they did. Charts and tables would provide excellent ways of recording their findings.

Drawing conclusions
The children should be able to establish from their results what they now know about each sample of rock. They should be able to put the rocks into some basic order of hardness or absorbency. Like scientists the children should have begun to build up a picture of something about which they originally knew little.

The teacher should record the main findings of the class and make a display including the rocks.

Children should be encouraged to use the real names of the rocks wherever possible.

There may be buildings or walls constructed from the rocks you have been observing near to the school. If so, bring them to the attention of the children so that they begin to understand that rocks are used in construction. Perhaps their findings will help them to see why a particular rock was used for that construction, for example, because it is hard or because water cannot enter it. Likewise the property of a rock may influence how it is used, for example, graphite for pencils, chalk for the blackboard and diamonds for drills.

Reference
An excellent publication for work on rocks is *Exploring Earth Science*, published by Northamptonshire Science Resources.

Assessment

ATTAINMENT TARGET 1

To assist teachers in undertaking assessments when children are undertaking scientific investigations the following support has been compiled. It sets out suggestions of the types of responses that teachers might observe when children are undertaking this investigation. Suggestions have been set out against levels 3 to 5 but it should be recognised that there may well be children who are working outside of these levels.

at level 3

Respond to suggestions
- The children could explain how they would set about investigating the hardness of the different rocks they had been presented with. After touching the rocks and discussing each one with their partners they predicted the order of hardness of the rocks.
- The children, with some help from the teacher, devised a number of ways of testing for hardness. They placed each in order, from 'will scratch with fingernail' to 'does not mark when scratched with a metal coin'.

Use equipment and make observations
- The children used magnifiers to look closely at the degree to which each rock had been marked.
- Observations of 'damage done' were clearly set down and recorded in written form and as observational drawings.

Carry out a fair test
- The children took great care to ensure that each test was carried out in the same way, that is, when scratching with either a fingernail or a coin, the same strength was used.

Record
- Charts were drawn with sketches made of each rock. Underneath each drawing the children had set down their observations. At the end of the investigation the children set out the rocks, in order of hardness, on a display at the side of the classroom. Incorporated into their display were all the children's sketches and records.

Explain observations
- The children used the display they had set up to explain to the class what they had done and what they had observed.

Is it what they expected?

■ The children explained that they had predicted the hardness of each at the beginning and although they were mostly right there were two rocks which were nearly the same hardness. On these two rocks they had had to observe the marks made under a very strong magnifier to discover which rock was the hardest.

at level 4   Recognise need for a fair test

■ The children explained that each rock would have to be left in the water for the same amount of time to test how absorbent each rock was.

Make predictions

■ The children said that they had found it difficult to predict which of the rocks were most absorbent because they did not think that rocks absorbed water. However, one rock was softer to touch than the others and so they thought that this would be the most absorbent.

Select apparatus

■ The children selected the tank and measuring equipment required to set up the absorbency investigation.

Recording

■ Graphs were made showing how much water had been absorbed by each rock.

Interpreting data

■ The children could, by reference to their records, explain which rocks were the most absorbent.

Drawing conclusions

■ Some children said that the 'softest' rocks were the most absorbent and others that the rocks with cracks in absorbed the most water in their investigation. None of their conclusions matched but all were based upon their recordings.

at level 5   Identifying key factors

■ The children identified that the amount of time each rock was in the water for was important as well as ensuring the same amount of water was placed in the tank each time.

■ They explained that the rocks couldn't stay in the water overnight as the water would evaporate and the investigation would not be fair.

Make predictions based upon scientific knowledge

■ The children predicted: *The clay will soak up the most water because when we made clay pots and the clay went hard we placed more water on it to make it softer.*

Select apparatus and use with precision

■ The children selected all the appropriate apparatus for setting up the absorbency investigation. They used electronic scales to weigh each rock before, and after to weigh the amount of water each rock had absorbed.

Make observations or measurements

■ The amount of water used was carefully measured using measuring jugs. The amount of water absorbed was noted by measuring the amount left when the rock was removed.

■ Checks were made by weighing each rock before and after being placed in the water.

Repeat and explain differences they encounter

■ They carried out the investigation again but this time they ensured that each rock was completely covered. They noticed that each rock now absorbed more water. Some explained that this was because more of the rock area was taking in water.

Recording

■ Careful records were made and comparisons drawn between the results when the rocks were weighed and when the amount of water left was measured.

Drawing conclusions

■ Children explained what they had discovered as a result of undertaking the investigation. Their conclusions were based upon the data that they had collected.

MATERIALS AND THEIR PROPERTIES

2. CHANGING MATERIALS

MATERIALS AND THEIR PROPERTIES

Work on solids, liquids and gases should be related to pupils' observations of changes that take place when materials are heated and cooled, and to ways in which mixtures can be separated.

Pupils should be taught:

2. Changing materials

a that mixing materials, *eg adding salt to water*, can cause them to change;

b that heating or cooling materials, *eg water*, *clay*, *dough*, can cause them to change, and that temperature is a measure of how hot or cold they are;

c that some changes can be reversed and some cannot;

d that dissolving, melting, boiling, condensing, freezing and evaporating are changes that can be reversed;

e about the water cycle and the part played by evaporation and condensation;

f that the changes that occur when most materials, *eg wood*, *wax*, *natural gas*, are burned are not reversible.

SCIENCE ACTIVITIES

Before setting up the investigation, children will need to have undertaken the following activities. The activities provide the children with the opportunity to acquire the skills and knowledge they will require in order to undertake the investigation. Preparing children with the appropriate skills and knowledge will assist the teacher's organisation of the investigation.

Whilst the children are undertaking the activities the teacher should plan to develop a vocabulary with which the children can work.

ACTIVITIES   Changing materials

CHANGES IN DOUGH

RESOURCES	Flour, water and yeast for making dough
Class or group discussion	Explain to the children the ingredients for making dough. Explain where each ingredient comes from and explain that by mixing the ingredients together each has an effect on the others. Explain these effects to the children.
Class demonstration !	Show the children how to mix their dough taking care to explain the amounts used and the health factors in keeping utensils clean and ensuring hands are clean before starting work.
Practical	Children investigate what happens when equal portions of dough are baked for different lengths of time. The children discuss things like colour, texture and size. They could compare the inside of the dough to the outside.
	Children should be developing an understanding that materials can be converted into new and useful products by chemical reaction.

2 CHANGES IN JELLY CUBES

RESOURCES	A collection of jelly cubes, thermometers, mixing bowls, wooden spoons for stirring and hot water stored in a thermos flask

Look at the jelly cubes and discuss with the children how they can dissolve them. Give clear instructions on how to dissolve the cubes. What volume of water will be used and how will they record the temperature of the water? How will they know when the cube has dissolved? What will they use to measure the time it takes for the jelly to dissolve?

This activity can be undertaken as a simple observational task which looks at how a solid dissolves and then resets; or it can be tackled as a simple investigation. If undertaken as an investigation it will introduce the children to the need for careful planning in setting up and carrying out an investigation. The children could explore whether the jelly melts at a different rate if the mixture is stirred. Each group could stir for a given length of time and record and compare the results. One group will need to simply place the jelly in the water and not stir at all to act as a control.

Practical   Use this investigation to encourage the children to consider how to set up a fair test:
- do we all have the same volume of water?
- is everybody's jelly the same size?
- how do we stir the mixture at the same rate?
- how do we decide when the jelly has dissolved?

! The children melt the jelly using hot water. This requires close teacher supervision.

The children explain what happens to the jelly and where it goes. They also discuss how the jelly cube has changed.

The children could investigate how long it takes jelly to set. Is it the same wherever the jelly is put?

3

CHANGES IN CLAY

RESOURCES

A plentiful supply of clay

Cross-curricular links ART

Children handle the clay and model simple shapes and objects. The children can describe how the clay feels. This simple investigation could be undertaken in an art lesson where children are introduced to the techniques of working with clay.

Encourage the children to note the differences between the clay before and after hardening. They should weigh the models as soon as they are finished and then draw simple sketches which include accurate measurements of the dimensions. The same measurements should be taken once the clay models have hardened. Have their models changed in any way? Encourage the children to record what they have observed and why they think the changes have taken place.

Children should be encouraged to link what they have discovered to examples around them. For example, cracks in plaster that appear on walls after a period of drying.

The children could go on to find out about the effect of heat on clay – by modelling and firing their own pots.

4

CHANGES IN BREAD

RESOURCES

A sliced loaf and a toaster with a timer

Class discussion

Discuss changes that occur when bread is toasted.

Practical

Toast a number of slices of bread for different periods of time.

Children are encouraged to observe closely, using a variety of senses, a slice of bread. What does it weigh? What is its area? How does it taste? The teacher could pose a question to encourage the children to discover what happens to the texture, taste, mass and area of a slice of bread after toasting. Toast slices of bread for different time periods and record the effect it has – through drawings and writing.

5

BURNING

RESOURCES

A burning candle

Class or group discussion

Discuss with the children what a candle wick needs in order to burn. The discussion could lead to children identifying the constituent parts of air.

Class demonstration

The teacher could demonstrate that oxygen is needed for the burning process to occur. This could be done by placing a jar over a burning candle. When the oxygen is used up the candle will go out.

The amount of oxygen in the jar can be estimated by placing a jar over the candle standing in a saucer of water. The height the water rises in the jar gives an indication of how much oxygen has been burnt.

what is lost?

Emphasise that the burning process has led to the loss of material and that the process cannot be reversed. The children will suggest that through burning the wick, the wax and the oxygen have been lost forever. The work can be followed up by a discussion on the effects of burning on the loss of gas or woodland.

6 DISSOLVING AND EVAPORATION

RESOURCES Warm water and salt

Practical activity Children can measure out a set amount of warm water and stir salt into it. The children should try to ensure that they do not try to dissolve too much salt into their water. Enough to ensure that as little salt as possible can be seen at the bottom of the warm water. Pour the salt solution onto shallow saucers and leave at the side of the classroom. Observe and record how long it takes for the water to evaporate, to 'disappear'. Observe the salt that is left behind. Develop the understanding that dissolving is a process that can be reversed.

Relate the dissolving process to applications in industry: salt is extracted from underground by pumping water into rocks containing salt.

 7 FREEZING

RESOURCES A fridge. A thermos flask for storing ice cubes in

Practical Children can measure out a set amount of water that they are going to freeze into ice cubes. Allow the children to freeze the ice cubes in the fridge if there is one in school. Collect up the ice cubes once they have melted and store in a thermos flask. The ice cubes can be allowed to melt in the classroom and the water measured.

Children should be developing an understanding that freezing is a process that can be reversed.

Relate the freezing process to everyday situations such as the freezing of a river or a water tank in a house. How is the process reversed?

 8 EVAPORATION AND CONDENSATION

RESOURCES A number of large, clear, plastic sweet jars. Compost and a collection of small, easy-to-grow plants

Practical In groups children can make their own micro-environment where they can observe evaporation and condensation taking place.

Place the sweet jar on its side and place some soil in the bottom – so that it is just below the lip of the jar. Plant your plants into the soil starting at the far end of the jar. Once the jar is full of plants then pour water into the soil. You can observe the amount of water you are placing in the jar by observing the level rise through the soil. Mark the final water level clearly on the side of the jar. Once there is sufficient water in the jar screw the cap on and leave.

As the mini-environment heats up and cools through the day the children will be able to observe evaporation and condensation taking place. They can observe the changing water level on the side of the jar.

Children can take responsibility for looking after their environment and ensuring it contains sufficient water and that the plants remain healthy. The work can be linked with work in geography on care of the local or world environment.

THE WATER CYCLE

A diagram of the water cycle. Better still would be a video or television programme which explains the water cycle

The children should have studied weather changes over time. They should also have studied the processes of evaporation and condensation. They could have this explained as the classroom windows steam up one day.

Children should also have been introduced to the idea of cycles. (Food chains Key Stage 2, Living things in their environment.) Once these have been explained children enjoy setting out cycles that they have thought of themselves.

Class or group discussion The teacher should explain that the water cycle is made up of four parts:
1. Evaporation of water takes place from large surface areas of water and forms water vapour.
2. Clouds are formed from this water vapour and are carried by air currents until they meet the cold temperatures over mountainous regions.
3. Condensation occurs, water droplets form and water begins to fall as rain.
4. Water is then transported by rivers and streams back to the sea and the process begins once again.

Practical Children can draw their water cycle. More able children will be able to include specific mountains, seas and rivers based upon their own knowledge or work covered in geography.

INVESTIGATION   Changing materials

"What affects the speed at which plaster of Paris sets?"

Resources
- plaster of Paris mix
- water
- heat source
- suitable mixing bowls (not those used for food)
- old spoons
- plaster of Paris cast
- moulds
- stop clocks
- thermometers
- scales
- measuring cylinders

Starting point
A Plaster of Paris cast.

Observing and asking questions
Children could discuss the plaster of Paris cast and what it is used for. Where have the children seen them used? Why are they used? Discuss how they think the cast was made. Look at the powder and discuss with the children what they think is needed to make the cast.

Children may ask
Does the temperature of the water affect how quickly the plaster of Paris sets?
Does the amount of water used affect how quickly the plaster of Paris sets?
Does the quantity of plaster of Paris powder affect how quickly the plaster of Paris sets?

Predicting
Encourage the children to make a prediction about what they think will happen and why. Children at Key Stage 2 will have considerable knowledge to draw upon from work undertaken by Key Stage 1 and could be encouraged to relate their predictions to relevant prior knowledge. Where have they seen previously things that solidify, and what seemed to affect the speed at which solidification took place?

Designing and planning the investigation
Encourage the children to set up a fair test. They should understand what to change and what to keep the same.

Water temperature   Children need to choose appropriate masses of powder and volumes of water to investigate. These will need to be kept constant in each test. They will need to decide the range of temperature they will be investigating so that they get significantly different results. They will also need to decide how many times the mixture will be stirred.

! Close supervision will be needed when water is heated.

Water volume   Children need to choose appropriate masses of powder and the temperature of the water. These will need to be kept constant in each test. They will also need to decide what volumes of water they will be investigating so that they obtain significantly different results. They will need to decide how many times the mixture will be stirred.

Mass of powder   Children need to choose appropriate masses of powder to investigate to ensure they obtain significantly different results. The temperature of the water will need to be kept constant in each test. They will also need to decide what volume of water they will be using in each test. They will need to decide how many times the mixture will be stirred.

The children will need to decide what equipment to use.

! Decisions need to be made as to where the investigation should take place. Safety needs to be considered at all times – particularly with the use of hot water.

The children will need to decide what jobs individuals will undertake within the investigation.

Be careful not to pour any plaster of Paris mixtures down the sink.

Recording

At the planning stage of the investigation the children will need to decide at what point they consider the plaster of Paris to be 'solid'. This decision will have a bearing on the results that are recorded. Will the children simply give a constant time limit during which the mixture will have set or give criteria that the mixture must fulfil before it can be considered to be solid? For example, the point at which the plaster will not take a thumb print (this may take too long). The children will need to decide how well they can record their findings so that definite conclusions can be drawn.

Drawing conclusions

The children should relate the results to their original idea. Every effort should be made to encourage the children to relate their findings to the data they have collected.

From the data they have collected is it possible for them to predict what would have happened if they had made other measurements? For example, is it possible to predict the speed of setting for a mass of powder that has not been tested simply by reference to the patterns in the data the children have collected?

As follow-up work could the data the children have collected inform real-life situations in hospital? Contact your local hospital to find out how plaster of Paris casts are made.

Assessment

ATTAINMENT TARGET 1

To assist teachers in undertaking assessments when children are undertaking scientific investigations the following support has been compiled. It sets out suggestions of the types of responses that teachers might observe when children are undertaking this investigation. Suggestions have been set out against levels 3 to 5 but it should be recognised that there may well be children who are working outside of these levels.

at level 3 **Respond to suggestions**
- The children could explain how they would set about investigating whether the temperature of the water they mix with the plaster affects the time it takes to set.
- They predicted that the plaster would set faster in warm water because the jelly they mixed set more quickly in warm water.

Use equipment and make observations
- They measured the amounts of water using standard measures and appropriate measuring jugs. They didn't use thermometers as they decided to use only cold and warm water straight from the taps.

Carry out a fair test
- They ensured that the same amount of plaster is used each time.

Record
- The children recorded their findings and produced a block graph showing the different rates at which the plaster set.

Explain observations
- The children could use their graph to explain clearly what happened and at which temperature the plaster set fastest.

Is it what they expected?
- The children could link what they discovered to what they had predicted saying whether their prediction was correct or not.

at level 4 **Recognise need for a fair test**
- They recognised that the amount of plaster needs to be the same each time.
- They decided that the plaster was set once you could not make a mark in it by pressing your finger onto it.

Make predictions
- The children could explain how they would set about investigating whether the temperature of the water that the plaster is mixed with affects the rate at which it sets.
- They predicted that the plaster would set faster in cold water because you wouldn't have to wait for the plaster to cool down. The piece of plaster that they observed they said felt cold.

Select apparatus
- They used a thermometer to ensure that they had accurate temperatures for the four amounts of water they used.

Recording
- The children collected the data and produced a graph of their results.

Interpreting data

■ The children could explain the different rates at which the plaster set and what their data indicated was the temperature at which plaster set quickly. They explained that they could explore the temperatures around the one that they found allowed the plaster to set quickly in order to find a more accurate measurement.

Drawing conclusions

■ The children drew conclusions which were explained by reference to their recordings.

at level 5

Identifying key factors

■ They identified temperature as the factor to be varied and could explain that the amount of plaster, the mixing bowl and the amount of water should be kept constant throughout.

Make predictions based upon scientific knowledge

■ They predicted that the warmer the water the faster the plaster would set because heated water allowed the powder to dissolve more quickly so that it mixed together prior to cooling and setting. They explained that they thought that the heating and cooling process used to mix the plaster is the same as that used when they made jelly and when they dissolved salt in cold and warm water.

Select apparatus and use with precision

■ Thermometers were used to measure the temperature of the water.
■ When the experiment was repeated they used timers correctly to measure time taken for the plaster to set.

Make observations or measurements

■ They made careful measurements of the time taken to set and could observe any patterns to their recordings.

Repeat and explain differences they encounter

■ They repeated the exercise but this time they recorded the amount of time it took for each amount of plaster to set. They were interested in looking at the relationship between time and temperature of water.
■ They constructed a line graph showing the temperatures and time taken to set. They looked for patterns and any differences that they encountered from the previous investigation.

Recording

■ Careful records were maintained throughout which were used as reference by the children to explain the different rates at which the plaster set.

Drawing conclusions

■ Their conclusions were based upon their recordings.
■ The children extended their graph in an attempt to predict the time it would take for the same amount of plaster to set at higher and lower temperatures. They explained how they would set about investigating if their predictions were correct.

MATERIALS AND THEIR PROPERTIES

3. SEPARATING MIXTURES OF MATERIALS

MATERIALS AND THEIR PROPERTIES

> Work on solids, liquids and gases should be related to pupils' observations of changes that take place when materials are heated and cooled, and to ways in which mixtures can be separated.

3. Separating mixtures of materials

Pupils should be taught:

a that solid particles of different sizes, *eg those in soils*, can be separated by sieving;

b that some solids, *eg salt*, *sugar*, dissolve in water to give solutions but some, *eg sand*, *chalk*, do not;

c that insoluble solids can be separated from liquids by filtering;

d that solids that have dissolved can be recovered by evaporating the liquid from the solution;

e that there is a limit to the mass of solid that can dissolve in a given amount of water, and that this limit is different for different solids.

SCIENCE ACTIVITIES

Before setting up the investigation, children will need to have undertaken the following activities. The activities provide the children with the opportunity to acquire the skills and knowledge they will require in order to undertake the investigation. Preparing children with the appropriate skills and knowledge will assist the teacher's organisation of the investigation.

Whilst the children are undertaking the activities the teacher should plan to develop a vocabulary with which the children can work.

ACTIVITIES — Separating mixtures of materials

SIEVING

RESOURCES — Different sized sieves. Soil that contains particles of different sizes. A bag of mixed gravel and stones of different sizes

Practical — Provide challenges for the children to separate out the large pieces of stone from the mixture or to collect the fine soil from the sample provided. Provide opportunities for children to develop an understanding that solid particles of different sizes can be separated by sieving.

DISSOLVING

RESOURCES — A collection of solids, some of which will dissolve in water. Include samples of salt, sugar, sand, chalk and gravel. Warm water stored in a thermos flask

The dissolving activity can help develop an understanding of how to undertake a scientific investigation. It is a simple and easy-to-manage investigation that the teacher can direct at each stage. In undertaking the investigation the children will be developing an understanding that will better equip them to plan and organise their own investigations.

Group or class discussion — Recap on what a solid is and how it differs from a liquid and a gas. Explain to the children that you have gathered together a collection of solids for them to investigate. Discuss how you might set up an investigation to find out which of the solids will dissolve in water. How might the children ensure that the investigation is fair? They may suggest that the same amount of water should be used each time and that the water is always warm (you don't need to be too exact about the temperature of the water as it will make the investigation difficult to organise within the classroom environment).

Useful tip — It is important to decide how each group will know that the water cannot dissolve any more sugar or salt. Explain that after they have stirred the solution they should wait for say three minutes and then check to see if they can see any solid particles in the water. If they can then the water cannot dissolve any more salt or sugar.

Recording — It is important to ensure that the children record carefully what they did and what they observed. Ask each group to explain what their recordings show.

Children should be developing an understanding that there is a limit to the amount of solid that can be dissolved in a given amount of water and that this varies for different solids.

THE SEWAGE FARM

RESOURCES — A visit to a sewage farm

At the farm — Children should find out how the water is cleaned for safe use.

Practical — Once back in school the children could investigate ways of purifying dirty water, using different materials. The emphasis should be on the use of filtration as a method of purification.

Children can set up filtering systems by taping together two plastic bottles (one with the base pierced), and placing materials that they feel will filter dirty water by acting as a 'sieve', at the join (see Figure 2). Discuss how the dirty water will be 'produced' so that it is the same for everybody and comparisons can be made on the way different materials filtered the water.

Children could research water cleanliness in other countries and the need for careful use of water.

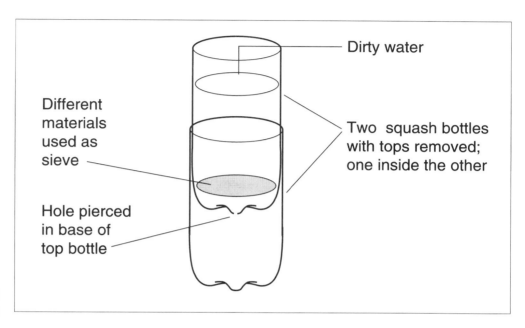

Dirty water

Two squash bottles with tops removed; one inside the other

Different materials used as sieve

Hole pierced in base of top bottle

Figure 2
A simple filter apparatus

 CHROMATOGRAPHY

RESOURCES

A collection of black water-based felt-tip pens. Blotting or filter paper

Practical

Write a number of messages on absorbent paper, preferably blotting or filter paper.

Take one of the messages and drip a small amount of water onto one of the words using a dropper. Show the children how the black spreads out and forms a range of colours. Explain that the range it creates is distinct to that pen.

Can the children match up the black felt-tip pen used to write the message?

This will involve the children creating the colour pattern for each pen and each message and then matching them up.

Discuss with the children the fact that the black ink in the pen is made up of a number of colours and that by dripping water onto it it breaks up into the mixture of colours that were used to create it in the first place. This splitting of colour into its component parts is called 'chromatography'.

Children could research what they can about chromatography and its uses.

MIXTURES

RESOURCES | Mixtures prepared by the teacher including mixtures of two solids, two liquids and a liquid and a solid. Useful mixtures include:

- sand and sugar;
- iron filings and sand;
- sugar and water;
- flour and water;
- olive oil and water;
- liquid soap and water.

Before this activity is undertaken children should have undertaken work to develop their understanding of filtration and evaporation (see next paragraph). The teacher should also have explained by demonstration how certain liquids can be separated by decanting. To demonstrate decanting it is important to have a container that pours without spilling and to have a steady hand.

Class demonstration | To demonstrate evaporation a saucer of water can be left at the side of the room and the time taken for evaporation to occur measured. The teacher can demonstrate how the rate of evaporation can be increased and used to separate mixtures by mixing salt into a small amount of water and then boiling until all the water has evaporated and the salt is left behind. It is important that the teacher undertakes the demonstration and not the children.

Class or group discussion | Ask the children to explain what they know about the properties of each substance used in the mixtures in terms of where it comes from, whether it floats on or dissolves in water. Do not show the children the mixtures until after you have discussed the substances you have chosen to use. List all the properties they have identified for each substance.

Show the children the mixtures and discuss what they think each contains. Ask them to give reasons for why they think a certain mixture contains certain substances. Recap on the different methods the children have used to separate mixtures.

Practical | Once the children have discussed the mixtures ask if they can separate the mixtures. Methods of separating may include filtering, decanting and evaporating.

Children should use their knowledge of the properties of materials to help them.

Recording | Children should record the process they went through in order to separate the mixtures and explain how successful each method was. The children may well attempt to separate a number of mixtures so that they develop a greater understanding of the processes involved and how it is important that the most appropriate method should be applied to separating the mixtures. The most appropriate method can only be decided upon by drawing upon previous knowledge of the properties of each substance in the mixture.

Class or group discussion | Children should be given the opportunity to discuss the most appropriate methods used for separating the substances. They should also be given the opportunity to relate the work to processes in industry and everyday life.

INVESTIGATION Separating mixtures of materials

"What affects the speed at which sugar granules dissolve in water?"

Resources
- granulated sugar
- brown sugar
- caster sugar
- icing sugar
- sugar cubes
- water
- kettle
- thermometer
- scales
- spoons
- heat-resistant containers
- beaker
- stop clocks

Starting point
A beaker of sugared water which the children taste. A discussion about where the sugar granules have gone could follow.

Observing and asking questions
The focus of the discussion should centre around what has created the sweet taste in the water and why it is that the sugar can no longer be seen. Before the children carry out any investigations it would be very useful for them to explore what happens to a variety of substances when they are added to water. For example, flour, sugar, salt, vegetable oil, liquid soaps, food colourings, golden syrup and bicarbonate of soda. The whole emphasis of this initial activity would be on the children exploring and discovering that some substances dissolve when added to water whilst others do not. Words such as 'suspension' could be introduced to explain those substances which do not dissolve. It is also interesting to see not only how solids react when added to water but also what happens to liquids, such as oil or washing-up liquid, when added to water.

A great deal of descriptive work and recording of observations could be done at this stage so that the children build up a bank of information to consult when they begin to think of questions they would like to investigate at a later stage.

 The children should be warned before any investigation begins of the dangers of tasting liquids unless they have been told that they are safe by an adult.

Children may ask
Does the colour of sugar affect how quickly it dissolves?
Does the amount of sugar affect how quickly it dissolves?
Does the amount of water affect how quickly the sugar dissolves?
Does the number of times the liquid is stirred affect how quickly the sugar dissolves?
Does the temperature of the water affect how quickly the sugar dissolves?
Does sugar dissolve more quickly than salt?

Predicting
The children should be able to make well-informed predictions about their investigations if they have undertaken a selection of previous activities from Key Stage 2. They may be able to make predictions which relate to the size of the granules of sugar. For example: *I think the icing sugar will dissolve more quickly than the granulated sugar because the granules are much smaller and the water will dissolve them quicker than the larger granules.* They may even suggest that the hotter the water the faster the sugar will dissolve because they have noticed this fact when adding sugar to tea.

Designing and planning the investigation
The children should be thinking very carefully about how they are going to ensure their investigations are fair. They will also need to consider what will be appropriate masses of sugar and volumes of water to work with so that they obtain reasonable results. If the children select inappropriate quantities the teacher will need to give careful guidance.

Type of sugar   In this investigation the children need to investigate at least three different types of sugar. All other aspects of the investigation should be kept constant – the mass of each type of sugar, the volume and temperature of water, the number of stirs and the container in which the dissolving is to take place. The children will need to decide when to start timing. For example, will it be as soon as they start to add the sugar to the water or will it be when they start to stir? They will also need to decide what they mean by 'completely dissolved', so that they know when to cease timing.

Mass of sugar   In this investigation the children will work with the same sugar type, temperature and volume of water, but they will change the mass of sugar. Careful choice of amounts should ensure that the results are significantly different to enable conclusions to be drawn and patterns to be identified.

Volume of liquid   This investigation will require the children to keep everything constant other than the volume of water being used.

Frequency of stirring   This investigation will require the children to keep everything constant other than the number of times each sample is stirred.

Sugar and salt   The properties of sugar and salt when added to water will be investigated. All other variables must be kept constant – the mass of sugar and salt, the volume and temperature of water, the number of stirs and the container.

Temperature of water   This investigation will need to be carefully supervised if the children have decided to investigate some high temperatures. They should select at least three different temperatures and these should be significantly different to provide meaningful results. All other variables should be kept constant. If the children are having difficulty reading the thermometer then they can be shown. Inaccurate reading of the thermometer by the children may affect the patterns in the data they have collected.

Recording

As each of the investigations is likely to involve timing, the use of graphs, charts and tables as methods of recording and presentation will be appropriate. It is important that the children are encouraged to use the data they have collected to inform their conclusions later on. The children should be encouraged to present their graphs and charts in a way that can be understood by others and they should meet the conventions associated with the presentation of graphs and charts.

Drawing conclusions

Using the data that they have collected the children should be able to draw very accurate conclusions from these investigations. Wherever possible they should relate their conclusion back to their original prediction and ask themselves whether or not they were correct. They should also be encouraged to look closely at each investigation to see if it was fair. If it was not, could it have had an effect upon the results? Another important question they could ask themselves is, did they take enough readings? Would they have obtained more reliable data if they had taken three readings at each temperature and worked out the range and mean for each test?

The more able children may begin to wonder if there is more than one thing that affects the rate at which sugar dissolves in water. They may begin to pose such questions as *Does the temperature of the water have more of an effect on speed of dissolving than type of sugar?* In order to answer such questions the children will need to consider the data collected from both investigations and draw a conclusion based upon those results.

Assessment

ATTAINMENT TARGET 1

To assist teachers in undertaking assessments when children are undertaking scientific investigations the following support has been compiled. It sets out suggestions of the types of responses that teachers might observe when children are undertaking this investigation. Suggestions have been set out against levels 3 to 5 but it should be recognised that there may well be children who are working outside of these levels.

at level 3

Respond to suggestions
- The children explained how they would set about investigating the rates at which the different substances dissolved in warm water.
- They predicted that the sugar lumps will dissolve more quickly because you get those at a cafe to dissolve in your tea.

Use equipment and make observations
- They measured the water using standard measures.
- They observed the different sugars dissolving and could time them accurately using timers.
- They observed the different rates at which each dissolved in the water.

Carry out a fair test
- They ensured that each sugar received the same number of stirs before timing the rate at which each dissolved.

Record
- They recorded their findings and produced a graph to show the different rates at which each sugar dissolved.

Explain observations
- They could, with reference to their data, explain what they observed.

Is it what they expected?
- They explained that what they expected was what happened but that one sugar, with fine granules, took longer than they expected and they didn't know why. They thought it might be because they had undertaken the test incorrectly so they went back and retested that particular sugar.

at level 4

Recognise need for a fair test
- They recognised that they would have to use the same amount of water at the same temperature and give each the same number of stirs.

Make predictions
- They predicted that the icing sugar would melt more quickly because it is finer than the others.

Select apparatus
- They selected and used accurately timers and measuring jugs.
- They used thermometers accurately to measure the water temperature.

Recording
- They recorded their data to show clearly the different rates at which the sugars dissolved.

Interpreting data
- They could explain what they observed with reference to their recordings.

Drawing conclusions
■ The children explained that their recordings indicated that the finer the sugar the quicker it dissolved.

at level 5

Identifying key factors
■ The children identified that they were investigating the rate at which different sugars dissolve in warm and hot water. They knew that they had to keep the two temperatures constant and that they would have to ensure that they placed in each sample of water the same amount of sugar and give each the same number of stirs.

Make predictions based upon scientific knowledge
■ They predicted that the substance with the finer granules would dissolve more quickly because this sugar has a greater area upon which the water can act to make it dissolve.

Select apparatus and use with precision
■ They selected the appropriate apparatus from a range available. They could measure time and temperature accurately.

Make observations or measurements
■ They recorded the time which each sugar took to dissolve at a set temperature. They gathered their data using appropriate measuring equipment.

Repeat and explain differences they encounter
■ The children had extended their line graphs to make predictions of the rates at which different sugars would dissolve at different temperatures. They tested out their ideas by selecting two temperature readings from their graph.

Recording
■ They presented line graphs showing the rates at which each sugar dissolved. They had extended their line graphs to try to predict the rates at which different sugars will dissolve at different temperatures.

Drawing conclusions
■ They drew conclusions based entirely upon their recordings. They looked for patterns and could explain clearly where patterns did or did not exist.

KEY STAGE 2

UNIT OF WORK

9

PHYSICAL PROCESSES

1. ELECTRICITY

PHYSICAL PROCESSES

The relationship between forces and motion should be made clear. It should also be made clear that both light and vibrations from sound sources travel from the source to a detector. Work on the Earth's place in the solar system should be related to pupils' knowledge about light.

Pupils should be taught:

1. Electricity

simple circuits

a that a complete circuit, including a battery or power supply, is needed to make electrical devices work;

b how switches can be used to control electrical devices;

c ways of varying the current in a circuit to make bulbs brighter or dimmer;

d how to represent series circuits by drawings and diagrams, and how to construct series circuits on the basis of drawings and diagrams.

ACTIVITIES

Electricity

ELECTRICAL CIRCUITS

RESOURCES A collection of electrical items including 1.5 V 'C' batteries, 'C' and 2 'C' battery holders, different lengths of wire stripped at the end and the wire twisted, 3 V to 6 V buzzers, 2.5 V and 3.5 V round MES bulbs and bulb holders

A collection of other useful items including lollipop sticks, small lengths of softwood that children can press drawing pins into easily, drawing pins, paper clips, Blu-Tack, Sellotape, scissors and easy-to-use wire strippers. Ensure you have explained how to use the wire strippers safely.

Remind the children that batteries are a source of energy and recap on work covered at Key Stage 1 (pages 61–62). Show the children the electrical items and explain what each item does. Demonstrate simple techniques for connecting wire to the different electrical items. For example, always twist the ends of the wire to make it easier to make a connection. Use small squares of thick card on which to mount the circuits. Each item can be stuck to the board using Blu-Tack. The children will find it easier to see the complete circuit.

Practical Ask the children to make a complete circuit incorporating one of the electrical items. Once they have done this ask them to make an accurate drawing of the circuit to enable others to make the circuit.

Class discussion Show a completed circuit to the class and ask them to think of a way that they could get the electrical device to go on and off. Most children will explain that you can just keep connecting and disconnecting the wire from the battery. Explain that this is a simple switch. Can they design their own more effective switch?

Children should be encouraged to think of different designs for switches. Introduce action words to describe how a switch works such as: push, pull, slide, press, turn, twist and drop switches.

Practical Give the children time to add a switch to their circuits. It is useful to limit the items they can use to those listed in the Resources section. It helps with organisation and ensures that children are not overwhelmed by having too many items to choose from.

Children should be given time to demonstrate their switches and for others to suggest ways in which they might be improved.

Now ask the children if they can add more than one electrical item to their circuit.

Group or class demonstration Children may ask to use more than one battery in their circuits as they consider this will give them more energy to make additional items work. This should be encouraged but first teachers should show the effect of attaching more batteries to a circuit which is to light a bulb. As batteries are added, the bulb shines more brightly but eventually it goes out as the heat created by the electricity was too great and has burnt out the thin wire in the bulb. Once the thin wire (that the children can easily see in the bulb) has been broken, the circuit is no longer complete and does not work. Count up the number of batteries required to blow a bulb and point out that the children should use fewer batteries to prevent the bulbs from being blown.

Safety   Explain to the children that working with electrical items connected to 1.5 V batteries is not the same as working with mains electricity which can be very dangerous. Find time to discuss with the whole class the dangers of mains electricity.

2 MAKING SWITCHES

RESOURCES Drawing pins, small softwood strips that children can easily place drawing pins into, paper clips

Practical Ask each child to make a complete circuit incorporating a bulb that lights. Cut one strip of wire leading to the bulb in two and make bare the ends. Ask the children to name objects that could be placed across the wires that would allow the electricity to pass through and light the bulb.

Show the children the equipment available for making switches. Explain that you want them to make a switch that will allow them to switch their bulb on and off.

It is often easier to place the circuit onto a board using Blu-Tack so that connections are not continually coming apart.

Once a simple switch has been made ask each child to demonstrate.

Describe each switch by its movement ie, sliding, pushing and pressing switches. Ask the children to devise different types of switches.

Children can now be asked to design a switch for a specific purpose. They could make a lighthouse out of a large plastic bottle and fit their circuit into the design. Incorporate circuitry work and switches into Design and Technology projects.

Teacher resource Good reference books with ideas for making switches are 'Electricity Books 1 and 2' (see bibliography for details).

3 SERIES AND PARALLEL CIRCUITS

RESOURCES A 1.5 V 'C' size battery, several strips of wire with the ends stripped bare and the wire twisted, 2.5 V round MES bulbs and bulb holders. Ensure that all the bulbs are of the same size – it is written on the metal base of the bulb

Provide each group of children with enough equipment to light three bulbs at once. Ask the children to place all three bulbs into one circuit. You will find that the children usually make a series circuit.

Explain that there are two types of circuits and that they have just produced a series circuit. Demonstrate how to make a parallel circuit where three bulbs can be lit at once.

Ask each group to create a series and a parallel circuit that lights three bulbs. When complete ask the groups to create a circuit to light one bulb and to make a note of its brightness. What differences do they note about the brightness of the bulbs in the three circuits? They will have noticed that in a series circuit the three bulbs will each be a third the brightness of a single bulb in a circuit. In the parallel circuit they will have noted that each bulb is as bright as a single bulb would be. This is because each bulb is connected to the battery along its own circuit.

Ask the children to make a drawing of each of the circuits.

4 DRAWING CIRCUITS

RESOURCES A number of drawings of series and parallel circuits containing different electrical components

Explain that electrical circuits are usually drawn in a particular way so that they can be readily understood by anybody. They are called circuit diagrams. Explain the following symbols:

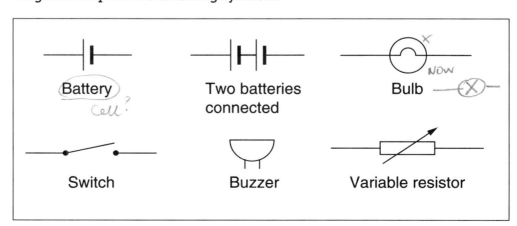

Figure 3
Electrical components

The wires on a circuit diagram are represented as four sides of a rectangle.

Practical Provide the children with drawings of a circuit that they have to build using the correct components.

Ask the children to make a circuit diagram that another group has to use to construct the circuit with the electrical components available.

Younger and less able children should work at the drawing stage.

5 BRIGHTER AND DIMMER BULBS

RESOURCES Resources are as for activity 3 plus a speed control switch kit (when inserted into a circuit this kit allows you to control the speed of a motor or acts as a dimmer switch for bulbs)

Practical Children can be introduced to the following ways of making bulbs brighter or dimmer:
■ connecting bulbs into a series or parallel circuit. See activity 3;
■ connecting a speed control switch into the circuit.
It is also possible to vary the light emitted from a bulb by connecting more batteries to the circuit or a different sized bulb. However, this can prove expensive as the bulbs will blow if too many batteries are connected. For instance if you use two 1.5 V batteries they will blow a 1.25 V bulb and so it is better to use a 2.5 V bulb if connecting more than one battery. It is a good idea to demonstrate the way a bulb can blow so that children do not attempt to do the same without changing to a 2.5 V bulb first.

Cross-curricular links DESIGN AND TECHNOLOGY Once the children are familiar with the different ways of varying the brightness of a bulb they can be provided with opportunities to apply their knowledge within design and making activities.

No investigation has been provided for this unit of work as it is not felt that work on electricity lends itself to a scientific investigation.

After having taught the activities set down for this unit teachers are advised to provide opportunities for children to apply the knowledge gained within a Design and Technology activity.

Children may apply their knowledge of electricity in undertaking one of the following Design and Technology activities:
■ attaching lights to a vehicle;
■ attaching lights to a shop window display;
■ making a flashing sequence to a set of lights to be attached to a fairground ride;
■ design and make a torch.

Further ideas for design and make activities can be found in: *Electricity Books 1 and 2* (Technology Teaching Systems); *Design and Technology – Primary Guidance* available from DATA (The Design and Technology Association), 16 Wellesbourne House, Walton Road, Wellesbourne, Warwickshire CV35 9JB, Tel: 01789 470007; and *Planning Primary Design and Technology* by Roy Richardson, published by John Murray Publishers.

PHYSICAL PROCESSES

2. FORCES AND MOTION

PHYSICAL PROCESSES

The relationship between forces and motion should be made clear. It should also be made clear that both light and vibrations from sound sources travel from the source to a detector. Work on the Earth's place in the solar system should be related to pupils' knowledge about light.

Pupils should be taught:

2. Forces and motion

types of force

a that there are forces of attraction and repulsion between magnets, and forces of attraction between magnets and magnetic materials;

b that objects have weight because of the gravitational attraction between them and the Earth;

c about friction, including air resistance, as a force which slows moving objects;

d that when springs and elastic bands are stretched they exert a force on whatever is stretching them;

e that when springs are compressed they exert a force on whatever is compressing them;

balanced and unbalanced forces

f that forces act in particular directions;

g that forces acting on an object can balance, *eg in a tug of war*, *on a floating object*, and that when this happens an object at rest stays still;

h that unbalanced forces can make things speed up, *eg an apple being dropped*, slow down, *eg a shoe sliding across the floor*, or change direction, *eg a ball being hit by a bat*.

SCIENCE ACTIVITIES

Before setting up the investigation, children will need to have undertaken the following activities. The activities provide the children with the opportunity to acquire the skills and knowledge they will require in order to undertake the investigation. Preparing children with the appropriate skills and knowledge will assist the teacher's organisation of the investigation.

Whilst the children are undertaking the activities the teacher should plan to develop a vocabulary with which the children can work.

ACTIVITIES

Types of force

RESOURCES	A good reference book for teachers is *Forces – A Guide for Teachers*, originally published by the NCC and obtainable from SCAA, Newcombe House, 45 Notting Hill Gate, London W11 3JB

Concepts	The concepts involved in the study of forces are:

- a force can start an object moving;
- a force can make an object move faster;
- a force can make an object slow down;
- a force can stop a moving object;
- a force can change the direction in which an object is moving;
- a force can change the shape of an object.

MEASURING FORCE

RESOURCES	A Newton meter

Force is measured in newtons on a Newton meter. A Newton meter (forcemeter) is a spring balance, calibrated in newtons (not kilograms).

Explain that forces can be measured using a forcemeter. Exhibit a forcemeter and demonstrate how it is used. Explain that scientists require a common unit for measuring forces so that tests can be fair wherever the scientist is working. Explain that force is measured in newtons.

Practical	Give the children an opportunity to use the forcemeter to measure forces. Ask them to record their results and compare them with the results of others to check the accuracy of their measurements.

MAGNETS

RESOURCES	A collection of magnets, both bar and horseshoe shaped. Ensure some of the bar magnets are coloured red and blue to show the North and South poles. A variety of different materials, some magnetic and some non-magnetic

It is important to make sure the children understand that magnets attract some materials but not others. Do not teach the children that magnets attract things that are made from metal.

Demonstration	Show the group the magnets and explain that they are made of a special metal that attracts certain materials. Explain that the ends are called poles. Show that some magnets are stronger than others by seeing how many paper clips each can lift.

Show how the magnets are attracted to each other but that the same poles will not attract. Explain that they push each other away – they repel each other.

Practical	Give the children a number of magnets and several materials in a container. Give them time to 'play' with the magnets and to feel the push and pull of the poles when brought together.

Ask the children to test which materials the magnets will attract. Ensure the children record their findings.

Gather the group together and see if everyone had the same results. Clarify, by demonstration, where children disagree so that it is clear which materials were and were not attracted by the magnets.

Set up a display where children can use magnets and reinforce their knowledge of the types of materials magnets do and do not attract.

3   GRAVITY

RESOURCES   Several small and light objects such as a fir cone or plastic ball. Ample supply of Plasticine

Teacher information GRAVITY

Newton stated that all objects attract other objects. Two objects lying on your desk are attracting each other but the force of attraction is very small. Nevertheless this attraction can be measured by scientists using specialised scales to measure these minute forces.

The force of attraction is determined by the mass of the object, ie the quantity of matter of which the object is composed. The greater the mass, the greater the attraction. The Earth has a great mass which exerts a force of attraction which pulls objects towards it. It is this force that gives objects their weight.

We would weigh less if we were to stand on the Moon because it has less mass than the Earth. Likewise we would weigh more if we could stand on Jupiter which has a much greater mass than the Earth.

The force of attraction exerted by the Earth is known as gravity.

The rate at which objects fall

The acceleration due to gravity does not depend on the mass of the falling object. This means that all objects fall at the same rate towards the centre of the Earth. This means that a light and a heavy object dropped from a tall building will hit the ground at the same time.

However, this does not always happen in practice as the fall of an object is affected by the air resistance acting upon it as it falls. The less streamlined object is affected most by the air resistance and so takes longer to hit the ground.

This means that to investigate the rate at which objects fall to the ground children will need to ensure that the objects they observe have the same shape.

Discussion

It is important to spend time discussing and explaining the principles outlined above. A good starting point for your discussion would be to view the experiment undertaken by the first men to land on the Moon where they dropped two objects and observed the rate at which they fell to the ground.

Practical

Ask the children to take one of the objects, a hollow plastic ball, and create the identical size shape from Plasticine. Standing on a chair drop the objects at the same time whilst other children observe when each hits the ground.

Children can repeat the activity using other objects.

Extension activity

Children could extend their investigation by observing the rate at which objects with the same mass but different shapes fall. This is difficult to do using Plasticine shapes as the height from which children can in practice drop their objects in the classroom is limited. However, children can observe the effect of changing the shape of objects with the same mass by using sheets of paper.

Take two sheets of A4 paper and crumple one into a ball. Drop the ball shaped paper and a flat sheet of paper from the same height and observe the different rates at which they fall. Children will enjoy making a number of different shapes out of A4 paper and predicting the rate at which each will drop to the floor. Encourage the children to record their results and provide opportunities for them to explain their findings to others.

FRICTION

RESOURCES

A brick, a board upon which the brick can be pulled, a Newton meter, wax or olive oil to create a slippery surface

Class or group discussion

Roll a toy vehicle across a smooth floor and across a carpeted area and ask the children to observe the different rates at which the vehicle travelled. Ask them to explain the reasons for the difference in the speed at which the vehicle travelled.

Explain to the children that friction slows down the rate at which an object travels.

Practical

Tie a piece of string around a brick so that a Newton meter can be attached. Explain how to use the Newton meter and that it is used to measure force. The groups are going to investigate the different forces required for a brick to travel across different surfaces. Choose several surfaces that can be placed on or created on the board. Ask the children to predict which materials will create the most friction and require the most force to get the brick to move. Rank the children's predictions and record them so that their predictions can be compared with their results.

Mark a line on your board and place the brick behind it. Hook your Newton meter to the string and pull until the brick begins to move. At this point take a reading on the Newton meter. Record the results.

Now pin smooth sandpaper to the board (too coarse and you could be waiting for a long time for the brick to move) and once again measure the force required to move the brick.

Children might suggest different surfaces to create on their boards. Wax can be spread across one section and polished to create a slippery surface.

Record their results and provide opportunities for the children to explain to others what they discovered. They should be encouraged to compare their findings with their predictions and to explain clearly what they discovered based upon their recordings.

STRETCHING AND COMPRESSING

RESOURCES

A wide selection of springs of different sizes. A wide selection of elastic bands of different lengths and thicknesses

Practical

Provide opportunities for children to experiment with the springs and elastic bands. They can use a Newton meter to measure the force required to stretch each over a given distance. If you do not have a Newton meter then simply attach a hook on the end of the band or spring and add weights until each is stretched the set distance and then count up the weight added.

Encourage the children to make predictions about which elastic band they think will require the most force to stretch it a given distance. Ask them to give reasons for their predictions. They may state that one band is thicker. Make a classroom display showing the children's findings. Ask the children to explain their findings and ensure that they explain their findings based upon their results and not on what they thought would happen – which may be very different.

Children should also be provided with opportunities to compress springs in order to feel the force being exerted by the spring. Children should be developing an understanding that the spring and elastic band exert a force which acts against the force which they are exerting. This concept can be related to the work undertaken in activity 3 'May the force be with you!' on page 144 where children exert opposite forces that create a balanced force.

ACTIVITIES

Balanced and unbalanced forces

FORCES

RESOURCES

A large selection of different objects that move or can be moved in different ways

Class or group discussion

Explain to the class that forces can act upon other forces of different sizes and directions and that a force can make an object change its speed or direction. Choose several of the objects you have collected and ask the children to think about the forces acting upon them. Discuss what they say and correct their ideas where appropriate. *Forces – A Guide for Teachers*, a booklet from SCAA, is a good reference for teachers undertaking this activity.

Practical

Ask the children to choose several of the objects and to explore how they work or move and to try to identify the forces acting upon them. The children should record their findings so that groups can compare results.

SPEED AND DIRECTION

RESOURCES

A collection of objects that move in different ways. A suitable collection could include: a boat with a sail that moves across water, a toy car, a marble, a football or netball, a 'pull-along' toy

Class or group discussion

Explain to the class that the size and direction of a force can affect the movement of an object. Choose several objects to explain exactly what you mean. Two different sized balls are probably the easiest way of explaining the principles involved but another example should be given that may not be so easy to understand, for example, a seed falling from a tree where the pull of gravity causes it to fall towards the ground with increasing speed.

Practical

Ask the children to choose several different objects and explore the way that force can affect speed and direction. Record their findings so that they can compare results with other groups.

The children should be developing an understanding that the greater the force the greater is the acceleration of the object. As far as is possible their investigations should be related to everyday situations such as road safety, cycling and sailing.

3   MAY THE FORCE BE WITH YOU!

RESOURCES

A physical education lesson – a large area in which to work and ample supplies of small PE apparatus

Scientific information

Explain to the children that a force is a push or pull and that forces can make an object move, speed up, slow down, stop, hold an object in place and change the shape of an object.

Practical

Children can begin by working in pairs during a physical education lesson to experience forces. They can push against each other's outstretched arms so that neither moves. Explain that the forces are equal and therefore balanced. Then ask them to carefully create an unbalanced force so that they move, slowly, around the room. The scientific terms 'balanced' and 'unbalanced' forces can be used as commands during this part of the lesson. Ask them, once they are moving slowly around the hall to increase the force. What has happened? Decrease the force. What has happened now?

Now group the children in fours with their hands outstretched and making a circle. Number each child from one to four. Whoever has 'The Force' moves the group. Call out numbers from one to four. Numbers can be called in pairs and the children told that each number has an equal force. What will happen when opposite numbers are called out? A balanced force is created. What happens when two numbers next to each other are called? What movement do the children see? Emphasise that forces can act in different directions and that forces of equal size in opposite directions will balance each other out.

Obtain a large rope and ask two children to pull the rope so that they have created a balanced force. Keep adding children but ensuring that the force is balanced. Now ask the children to do the same activities as when they were pushing against each other's arms. Children should be developing an understanding that forces can be balanced and unbalanced and are created by pushing and pulling.

Place small apparatus around the side of the hall. Include ropes, a selection of small balls, bats etc. Ask the children to create forces that make an object:
- move;
- speed up and slow down;
- stop;
- be held in one place;
- change its shape.

Can the children choose one object from the basket and demonstrate all the above effects?

Extension activity

The next PE lesson could concentrate upon creating unbalanced forces. An unbalanced force makes things speed up, slow down or change direction. Concentrate upon each one in turn and use the scientific terms 'force' and 'unbalanced' force.

4

SLOWING DOWN AND SPEEDING UP

RESOURCES

Photographs showing where friction has been used to slow things down or where friction has been reduced to increase speed. A pair of skis could be brought into the classroom to illustrate how smooth they are to cut down on the friction as they pass over snow and ice. Can the children think of ways of making them pass more quickly across the ice? Downhill skiers rub wax onto the base of their skis to cut down the friction and help them travel faster

There are a wide range of applications, many of which the children will be aware of. Once children have been given several examples they are very good at thinking of further examples.

The following is a list of examples to get you started:

Slowing things down using friction:
- a parachute;
- the brakes on any vehicle;
- a parachute to slow down a dragster.

Speeding things up by reducing friction:
- the clothing and cycling position of speed cyclists;
- the shape of modern cars;
- the shape of Concorde;
- swimmers wear bathing caps and shave their bodies;
- a catamaran which provides less surface area touching the water.

INVESTIGATION

Forces and motion

"What is friction, and is it always the same?"

Resources
- bricks of different mass
- forcemeter
- selection of materials with different surfaces
- string
- protractor for measuring angles

Starting point
Picture of ice skaters and a discussion about sliding on the playground.

Observing and asking questions
The children should be encouraged to express their ideas about why skaters find it easy to glide across ice. Also about why it is easier to slide on the playground in icy weather. Discussion could also centre around the design of grips on the soles of shoes, and certain surfaces which are made to be anti-slip. Reference could also be made to roads and stopping distances for cars.

The children need to know that forces can be measured using a forcemeter. Encourage the children to look closely at the bricks and materials that are on display. If the bricks are going to be pulled across different surfaces what do the children think will happen?

Children may ask
Is friction the same on every surface?
Does the weight of the brick affect the amount of force needed to move it?
Does a slope affect the amount of force needed to move a brick?

Predicting
Taking into account the points that they discussed about differences in the ease with which the bricks move across the different materials, which surfaces will allow the bricks to pass over them more easily? Consider the surfaces alone, not the bricks and surfaces together, as some children will find it difficult to look at more than one variable at once. Encourage children

to explain their reasons in a scientific way. They may well begin to use the terms 'force' and 'friction'. Record the children's ideas to refer to at the end of the investigation.

Designing and planning the investigation

Before carrying out the investigation the children as a class could put together ideas about how they might investigate the forces needed for a brick to move over a surface.

Ensure surfaces and equipment are on display to allow children to choose for themselves.

Some groups will need a considerable amount of teacher input, whilst others will work quite independently. The teacher should be encouraging the children to work as independently as possible in planning, setting out and carrying out their studies.

The more able groups could be asked to investigate what affects how a brick moves across different materials. This will involve them deciding for themselves what they are to explore and which variables they are going to control. They may wish to look at the mass of the brick, the amount of surface in contact with the brick, or how much a slope affects the force needed.

Surface type   In this investigation the brick used will be the same for each test but the surface under the brick must be different for each test. The children will attach the forcemeter and begin to pull. Once the brick moves the force on the meter will be recorded.

Brick mass   This investigation will require bricks of different mass. The surface under the bricks will be kept constant for each test.

Slope   This investigation will require the brick and surface to be kept constant, but the slope of the surface to be changed for each test. It would be best for children to measure the angle of the slope for each investigation.

Recording

Before the children begin their investigation they should understand clearly what they are setting out to investigate, what they need to record, and how. Whilst undertaking the investigation, their recordings can be in rough and can be copied out clearly at a later date.

The children should be deciding on the most appropriate method of recording their results so that others fully understand.

Drawing conclusions

Ensure that the children's findings are based upon their investigation and not on their initial predictions. Is there a difference and can they see reasons for these differences? With their findings children could now explore ways of reducing the force required to move a brick across a wooden surface. This will give the children the opportunity to investigate the effects of using different lubricants to reduce frictional forces.

Wherever possible link the children's work to real life situations. For example, the Egyptians reduced frictional forces on the stone blocks used to build the pyramids by placing rollers under them.

Assessment

ATTAINMENT TARGET 1

To assist teachers in undertaking assessments when children are undertaking scientific investigations the following support has been compiled. It sets out suggestions of the types of responses that teachers might observe when children are undertaking this investigation. Suggestions have been set out against levels 3 to 5 but it should be recognised that there may well be children who are working outside of these levels.

at level 3   **Respond to suggestions**
- The children could explain how they would set about investigating if different forces were required to pass a brick over different surfaces.

Use equipment and make observations
- They could set up the investigation and could use a forcemeter to measure accurately the force required to pull a brick over each of the surfaces.

Carry out a fair test
- The children ensured that the test was fair by using the same brick each time and by using the same side of the brick (same area in contact with the surface).

Record
- The children recorded their results in a chart form. They set up a display in the classroom on which they placed the various surfaces and their charts. They also placed the brick on one of the surfaces so other children in the class could use the forcemeter and check if the results they obtained were the same.

Explain observations
- The children used their display to explain their results to the rest of the class.

Is it what they expected?
- Their results were not exactly as they had expected. They explained what had happened that they had not expected and drew upon their recordings throughout.

at level 4   **Recognise need for a fair test**
- The children explained that they were going to investigate the angle of slope and its effect upon the force required to pull a brick down a slope.

Make predictions
- The children predicted that a greater amount of force would be required to pull the brick down the slope when the slope was less steep.

Select apparatus
- The children used a calibrated slope and could set it up and read off the angle of slope accurately.

Recording
- Block graphs were produced showing both the angle of slope and the force measured.

Interpreting data
- The children could explain to others what they had done and what they had found out referring constantly to the data they had collected.

Drawing conclusions
- They explained that the greater the slope the less the force required to move the brick.

at level 5   ### Identifying key factors

■ The children identified that the key factors within their investigation were the angle of slope, the brick and the surface that the brick would travel across. They explained that they would use the same brick and surface and change the angle of slope.

Make predictions based upon scientific knowledge

■ The children explained that as the slope became steeper the force of gravity pushing it down the slope would increase and so you would require less force to make the brick move.

Select apparatus and use with precision

■ They selected an interval of 20 degrees and started from the flat. They could measure the angle with accuracy using a large protractor.

Make observations or measurements

■ Measurements were taken at intervals of 20 degrees and the force applied was measured with accuracy using a forcemeter.

Repeat and explain differences they encounter

■ The children were enthusiastic to repeat the investigation but this time to pull the brick along on its narrow rather than its wide side to see if there was any difference.

■ They explained that they did not think that it would make any difference because the mass of the brick was the same no matter which way you pulled it along.

Recording

■ The children recorded their data accurately showing clearly the decrease in the force required as the angle of slope increased.

Drawing conclusions

■ They explained that their prediction had been correct (except for the prediction about the area of the brick in contact with the surface).

■ They looked for and identified any patterns in their recordings.

PHYSICAL PROCESSES

3. LIGHT AND SOUND

PHYSICAL PROCESSES

> The relationship between forces and motion should be made clear. It should also be made clear that both light and vibrations from sound sources travel from the source to a detector. Work on the Earth's place in the solar system should be related to pupils' knowledge about light.

Pupils should be taught:

3. Light and sound

everyday effects of light

a that light travels from a source;

b that light cannot pass through some materials, and that this leads to the formation of shadows;

c that light is reflected from surfaces, *eg mirrors, polished metals*;

seeing

d that we see light sources, *eg light bulbs, candles*, because light from them enters our eyes;

vibration and sound

e that sounds are made when objects , *eg strings on musical instruments*, vibrate but that vibrations are not always directly visible;

f that the pitch and loudness of sounds produced by some vibrating objects, *eg a drum skin, a plucked string*, can be changed;

g that vibrations from sound sources can travel through a variety of materials, *eg metals, wood, glass, air*, to the ear.

SCIENCE ACTIVITIES

Before setting up the investigation, children will need to have undertaken the following activities. The activities provide the children with the opportunity to acquire the skills and knowledge they will require in order to undertake the investigation. Preparing children with the appropriate skills and knowledge will assist the teacher's organisation of the investigation.

Whilst the children are undertaking the activities the teacher should plan to develop a vocabulary with which the children can work.

ACTIVITIES   Everyday effects of light

REFLECTION OF LIGHT

RESOURCES

Prisms, lenses, coloured filters, water tray, bottles (empty and full of water), reflective mirrors (not glass), torches, spare batteries and a collection of good reference books on light

Class discussion

The teacher should recap on work undertaken at Key Stage 1.

Practical

The children should be given the opportunity to explore the effect of light shining on or through lenses, mirrors and prisms. They should record their findings carefully so that they can compare the different effects of light shining on the different objects.

Explain to the children that it is the light being reflected off objects that enables objects to be seen. This is a very difficult concept for young children to understand and may be remembered but not fully understood. Primary teachers should not be concerned as this will be picked up and developed further at Key Stage 3.

It is very rare that children experience conditions of total darkness. On some visits to caves the guide will cut out all the lights to allow the children to experience total darkness.

Research

Give the children time to research into how rainbows are made, what prisms do to light, how light is made and how it travels to create images in our eyes. This work could be undertaken in an English lesson by using the jigsaw approach where a group of children research an area that they know little about, pool their findings and then record what they think are the most important aspects of what they have discovered. Allow time for the children to report back and help to clarify the more difficult aspects of the way in which light travels.

Practical

Once the children have gained a greater understanding that light is made up of the colours of the rainbow they can set about recreating the exact colours themselves. Once they are capable of recreating the colours of the rainbow they can make a colour wheel that can be spun and the children can observe how the colours combine to create white (see Figure 4) (a reversal of what happens when they see a rainbow being created).

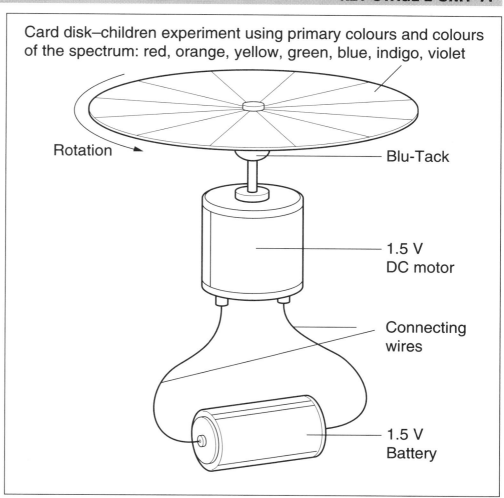

Card disk–children experiment using primary colours and colours of the spectrum: red, orange, yellow, green, blue, indigo, violet

Rotation

Blu-Tack

1.5 V
DC motor

Connecting
wires

1.5 V
Battery

Figure 4
Making a colour wheel

ACTIVITIES

Seeing

2

SEEING THE LIGHT

RESOURCES Torches, shoe boxes, card tubes, coloured card

Practical Cut two holes in the end of a shoe box and attach two lengths of card tubing to act as viewing holes – ensure they are the correct distance apart for the children to look through binocular-fashion. Make a slit in the lid at the far end of the box. Design several scenes that can be slid down at the end of the box. Cover or paint the inside of the box in black.

You will need to find as dark a place as possible to undertake this investigation. The children must be able to look through the tubes and be unable to see anything at the end of the shoe box. When a torch is lit then enough light will be available for the children to describe the scene placed at the end of the box.

Children should be developing an understanding that they can see light sources because the light enters their eyes.

3 LIGHT PASSING THROUGH OBJECTS

RESOURCES

Make a selection of materials, some of which allow light to pass through and some of which do not

Practical

Make a classroom display, setting out the variety of materials collected and a light source such as a torch. Provide opportunities for the children to classify the materials. The children will enjoy adding their own materials and discovering those that will or will not allow light to pass through.

ACTIVITIES Vibration and sound

1 MAKING MUSICAL INSTRUMENTS

RESOURCES

A collection of musical instruments, including a tuning fork

Group or class discussion

The following shall form the focus of any group or class discussion.
1. Sound travels through the air as waves that reach our ears.
2. Some materials are better than others for making sounds.
3. Sound waves can be reflected.
4. Volume can be increased with the addition of a 'sound box'.
5. Sounds can be made by making materials vibrate by plucking, stroking, banging.
6. Some materials absorb sound – as in a soundproof room. Many uncarpeted classrooms reflect sound and produce more noise than the children are actually making.

Class or group demonstration

Children can find it difficult to imagine sound waves travelling through the air and it will help their understanding if the waves could be made 'visible'. If you take a tuning fork and strike it against a hard object and then lower it slowly into a bowl of water the children will be able to see the waves spreading out from the vibrating fork.

Practical

Children should explore the ways in which they can control pitch, loudness and timbre by changing the characteristics of the vibrating object or altering the way in which it is made to vibrate. This can be undertaken with a collection of musical instruments or ones they have made themselves in Design and Technology.

Some children may find it easier to understand the principles involved if they make a simple plucking instrument by stretching an elastic band across a cardboard box. They will need some strips of wood to make bridges for the strings to rest on and to cut a hole in the box to create their own 'sound box'.

2 VIBRATIONS PASS THROUGH MATERIALS

RESOURCES

A window and a door of the classroom, a plank of wood, a swimming pool

Group or class discussion

Recap on work covered so far. Before undertaking the following activity children should have developed an understanding that:
■ sounds are made when objects vibrate;
■ that the vibrations cannot always be seen;
■ that it is these vibrations that reach our ears as sound.

Practical Explain to the children that they are going to explore if the vibrations from sound sources can travel through different materials. How will the children know if the vibrations have passed through a material? They will be able to hear the sound made.

Ask one child to take a musical instrument and to stand outside the classroom window. Stand another child on the other side of the closed window. Blindfold the child and ask him/her to listen carefully to hear and recognise the musical sound made. The same can be done for other materials, eg the closed classroom door.

If there is a long piece of wood available a child can place an ear to the wood and indicate when somebody taps on the other end of it.

If the class go swimming, one child can make a sound under the water at one end of the pool and the children at the other end can indicate if they can hear the sound. The teacher can remind the children of the long distances over which whales communicate with each other.

3

MAKING MUSICAL INSTRUMENTS IN DESIGN AND TECHNOLOGY

RESOURCES A collection of musical instruments that can be plucked or banged to create a sound

The musical instruments can be analysed by the children to identify the materials from which they were made, and how the sound is created and controlled.

Discuss the main parts required to make an instrument for plucking or banging. How is the volume of the sound controlled? How is the pitch controlled?

Practical Once the children have a clear understanding of the elements required of a musical instrument they can set about designing and making their own.

Extension activity The children could compose simple pieces of music to accompany a poem or part of a story. They could write a short play for assembly in which they use their musical instruments within the play. This could form the basis of their evaluation of their musical instruments.

INVESTIGATION Light and sound

"How does a guitarist change the sound his instrument makes?"

Resources
- elastic bands
- shoe boxes
- wooden blocks
- old guitar
- large cardboard boxes

Starting point
Observing somebody play a guitar.

Observing and asking questions
Discuss with the children how the sounds are made, how the pitch is changed and how the volume of the guitar is increased.

Children may ask
Does the thickness of the string affect the sound?
Does the length of the string affect the sound?
Does the size of the soundbox affect the volume?

Predicting
Encourage the children to make a prediction before carrying out their investigations and to give reasons for their predictions.

Designing and planning the investigation
Some children will undertake an investigation into the effect of changing the length of the elastic band (see activity 1 – Making musical instruments). This can be done by placing blocks of wood at different positions under the elastic band.

Some children will realise that the thickness of the band affects the pitch and may be able to investigate both thickness and length together and observe their effect on pitch.

Some will investigate volume by placing the same thickness of band over different sized boxes.

Some may realise that the force used to pluck the band affects volume and will look at ways of controlling the force to undertake a fair investigation.

Recording
This investigation will be difficult to record in any quantifiable way. However there is a sensor that can be attached to the BBC Microcomputer called the Panthera Measuring Box (obtainable from: 5 Cedar Avenue, Beeston, Nottingham NG9 2HA), which will give a screen display and print-out of the volume of sound created. The children will need to trust their ears to give judgement on pitch.

Drawing conclusions
Children should be encouraged to formulate their findings in scientific terms. *The pitch depends upon the length of the elastic band. The higher the pitch, the shorter the elastic band. The thicker the elastic band, the lower the pitch. The volume created depends upon the size of the soundbox. The bigger the soundbox, the greater the volume. The bigger the soundbox, the greater the sound when the elastic band is struck or plucked with the same force.*

The children's conclusions should be based upon their investigations which they should use to explain their findings.

Children could move on from this investigation to activity 1 where they make their own instruments on which to compose their own music.

Assessment

ATTAINMENT TARGET 1

To assist teachers in undertaking assessments when children are undertaking scientific investigations the following support has been compiled. It sets out suggestions of the types of responses that teachers might observe when children are undertaking this investigation. Suggestions have been set out against levels 3 to 5 but it should be recognised that there may well be children who are working outside of these levels.

at level 3

Respond to suggestions
■ The children explained how they might set about investigating the effects of different-sized boxes on the volume produced.
■ They predicted that the bigger the box, the greater the sound produced.

Use equipment and make observations
■ They observed the different volumes produced when placing an elastic band over a variety of different-sized boxes.
■ They used cutting and shaping tools to set up their investigation.

Carry out a fair test
■ They used a plucker to pluck the elastic band because they wanted to ensure that the elastic band was plucked with the same force each time.

Record
■ They recorded their findings in graph form.
■ They wrote up an explanation of what they did and what they found out based upon their recordings.

Explain observations
■ They could explain that their recordings showed that the larger the box, the greater the sound produced.

Is it what they expected?
■ They could explain whether what they predicted was what they found out based upon their recordings.

at level 4

Recognise need for a fair test
■ They recognised that the same-sized elastic band needs to be used each time. When they placed the bands over the boxes they observed that the pitch varied and they explained that they needed to try to keep it the same each time. They cut a hole of the same size in two different boxes and stretched the band to the same length over each box to ensure a fairer test.

Make predictions
■ They predicted that the larger box would produce the greater volume.

Select apparatus
■ They used appropriate apparatus from a range provided.

Recording
■ They recorded their results devising their own form of graph.
■ Their recordings were clear and easily understood by others.

Interpreting data
■ They could interpret their data and explained clearly to others what they found out.

Drawing conclusions

■ They could explain from their data which boxes produced the greater volume. They could explain that two similar sized boxes produced different volumes of sound and that you could clearly see where this did not fit any pattern on their graph. They explained that this could be due to the fact that the boxes are made from different materials.

at level 5

Identifying key factors

■ They identified that the boxes need to be made from the same materials and that the elastic band should be of the same length and thickness.

■ When they set up their investigation they ensured that the hole was of the same size and that the elastic band was stretched to the same length.

Make predictions based upon scientific knowledge

■ They noted that the boxes were not made from the same materials and predicted that one box would produce a greater volume than another of similar size because it was made from a denser material.

Select apparatus and use with precision

■ They selected appropriate equipment to take measurements and chose a calculator to work out the volume of each box.

Make observations or measurements

■ They measured the lengths of the sides of each box to calculate the volume of each.

Repeat and explain differences they encounter

■ They repeated their investigation but used the same-sized boxes made from different materials.

■ Their findings indicated that the volume of sound produced varied for each box. They explained that the size and the material that is used both affect the volume produced.

■ They explained that it is the density of the material used that affects the volume. The greater the density, the greater the volume. They chose two boxes of the same size but made from material of differing densities to test out their theory.

Recording

■ They produced line graphs showing the volume of the boxes in relation to the volume of sound produced.

Drawing conclusions

■ They drew conclusions from their recordings and related them to their knowledge of the density of different materials.

PHYSICAL PROCESSES

4. THE EARTH AND BEYOND

PHYSICAL PROCESSES

The relationship between forces and motion should be made clear. It should also be made clear that both light and vibrations from sound sources travel from the source to a detector. Work on the Earth's place in the solar system should be related to pupils' knowledge about light.

Pupils should be taught:

4. The Earth and beyond

the Sun, Earth and Moon **a** that the Sun, Earth and Moon are approximately spherical;

periodic changes **b** that the position of the Sun appears to change during the day, and how shadows change as this happens;

c that the Earth spins around its own axis, and how day and night are related to this spin;

d that the Earth orbits the Sun once each year, and that the Moon takes approximately 28 days to orbit the Earth.

SCIENCE ACTIVITIES

Before setting up the investigation, children will need to have undertaken the following activities. The activities provide the children with the opportunity to acquire the skills and knowledge they will require in order to undertake the investigation. Preparing children with the appropriate skills and knowledge will assist the teacher's organisation of the investigation.

Whilst the children are undertaking the activities the teacher should plan to develop a vocabulary with which the children can work.

ACTIVITIES   The Sun, Earth and Moon

THE MOON

RESOURCES	Model spheres showing how the Moon revolves around Earth
Group or class discussion	Observing the Moon.

Children could be encouraged to look whilst at home but may occasionally see it in the morning.

What is the Moon?
When can we see it?
Does it always look the same?

The children could keep a diary showing the shape of the Moon at different times in the month.

Class or group demonstration   The Moon revolves around the Earth in approximately 28 days. This could be demonstrated and discussed using model spheres.

Observation   Point out to the children that the Sun, Earth and Moon are approximately spherical, as can be seen by observing the Sun and the Moon.

2   'MY DAY'

RESOURCES   Charts on which to set down what each child does on a normal day

Group or class discussion   What things do you do in a day? (Examples might be: go to school, play, sleep).

The children could show with pictures or charts what they have done each day for a week. Then the teacher could invite the class to think how to show the times when it is night and the hours of daylight.

Are your days different in the summer or winter?

Set up records of the children's day and compare the activities they undertake, eg when do they go to bed, when do they get up? What do they do when it is dark? What do they do when it is light? What difference does it make to their activities when it is warm?

3   SUNDIALS

RESOURCES   A simple object, for example a length of stick, placed in the ground to cast a shadow

Discussion   Sundials made by the children can be discussed.

Why does the shadow move round the sundial?
When do we get long and short shadows?
What is the shortest period of time which it is possible to record on a home-made sundial?

Practical   Look at how shadows on the classroom wall move throughout the day. Could these shadows be used to give an approximate time of day? How?

The children could also study the sundial designs which are popular in gardens and on buildings, and evaluate which is the easiest to use and interpret.

 DAY AND NIGHT

RESOURCES   A torch, a large ball to represent the Earth and a small ball to represent the Moon

Group or class discussion   Explain to the children how the Earth rotates around the Sun, and the Moon around the Earth.

Use the torch to represent the Sun to explain how night and day are created by this movement.

What is happening to the Earth as it moves in space around the Sun?
How long does the Earth take to complete one spin on its own axis?
How long does it take for the Moon to travel around the Earth?
Which parts of the Earth are closest to the warmth of the Sun?

 THE SEASONS

RESOURCES   A torch and a sphere to represent the Earth

It is more realistic if the children can make a papier mâché Earth with the Equator clearly marked on it.

Class or group discussion   Use the model to explain to the children how the axis of rotation of the Earth is tilted with respect to its plane of rotation around the Sun. Use the torch to represent the Sun and show how the Earth rotates around the Sun. Explain how this determines day and night and length of day and the year.

Why are some parts of the world colder or warmer than others? How does the fact that the Earth's axis is tilted at an angle (66°) create the seasons?

Practical   The children could use the torch and model to explain to a friend how this tilt creates summer and winter.

How many hours of daylight and darkness do we have at different times of the year in the UK?
How can we find out? (Reference sources such as lighting up times in diaries and newspapers could be mentioned.)

INVESTIGATION The Earth and beyond

"What are shadows?"

Resources
- variety of objects that will create shadows
- rulers
- tape measures
- camera (not essential)
- video recorder (not essential)
- chalk

Starting point
A walk around the school on a sunny day.

Observing and asking questions
Initially look for all the shadows that can be found on your walk. Discuss with the children why shadows appear. The children could be encouraged to put out a variety of objects to see what shapes of shadows they create. Some children may suggest that the shadows will be different at different times during the day. This should lead to a variety of questions which could be investigated.

Children may ask
Do shadows get longer during the day?
Does the position of shadows change during the day?

Predicting
The children could predict what will happen in their investigations and give reasons. It may be possible for children to give reasons for their prediction which reflect quite a high level of knowledge. Some children may be aware that the position of the shadows will change because of the apparent movement of the Sun across the sky. It is unlikely at this stage that they will be aware that it is the Earth moving in relation to the Sun that affects the size and position of the shadows.

Designing and planning the investigation
The children will need to decide which places around school will be best for investigating shadows. They will also need to decide over what period they are going to observe them. If they are conscious that shadows in the summer are different to those in winter, then it may well be a very long-term investigation.

A good scientist makes sure that the investigation is a fair one.

If the children are unsure what is meant by fair investigation then you may need to explain. For instance, if they choose a summer and winter comparison, they must take care to ensure that they always do the same things at the same time each day.

Length and position of shadow   Both these investigations can be carried out at the same time. The children simply have to decide at what intervals they are going to record the length and position of the shadow.

Recording
The recording could be done as a group or as a whole class over a long time period. If the whole class undertakes the investigation then it can be easier for the teacher to manage but more difficult to undertake individual assessment.

This investigation allows the teacher to observe children choosing and using measuring and recording equipment. Teachers should ensure that the children have opportunities to choose their equipment.

Drawing conclusions
This aspect of the investigation is probably the most important as it will be at this stage that the teacher will need to try and draw out from the children what happened and why.

Hopefully the children will have begun to realise that the Earth is moving in relation to the Sun and that therefore our position on the Earth changes in relation to the Sun throughout the day.

This activity is an excellent introduction to the idea of the Earth's position in the Solar System and how the Earth moves around the Sun once a year.

Assessment

ATTAINMENT TARGET 1

To assist teachers in undertaking assessments when children are undertaking scientific investigations the following support has been compiled. It sets out suggestions of the types of responses that teachers might observe when children are undertaking this investigation. Suggestions have been set out against levels 3 to 5 but it should be recognised that there may well be children who are working outside of these levels.

at level 3

Respond to suggestions
■ The children could, in discussion with the teacher, explain how they would set up an investigation to explore the shadows cast from stakes of different length throughout the day.

Use equipment and make observations
■ The children used metre rulers to measure the shadows each week.

Carry out a fair test
■ The children explained that they had to make sure the stakes were not moved as the test would not be fair if they were placed somewhere else.

Record
■ Over a period of time the children have kept careful records which they have made into a chart to show the length of the shadow from each stake.

Explain observations
■ They explained that the shadows were different because the Sun moves during the day. Their recordings showed that the shadows were longer in the mornings as the Sun was lower in the sky.

Is it what they expected?
■ The children explained that they had not expected the shadows to vary so much during each sunny day.

at level 4

Recognise need for a fair test
■ The children explained that measurements must be made at the same time of day each week.

Make predictions
■ The children predicted that the shadows would be different in length during the day but the same at the same time each successive day.

Select apparatus
■ They selected an appropriate instrument for measuring the length of each shadow from a range to hand.

Recording
■ Weekly records were kept and information was used to compile a simple graph to show their results.

Interpreting data
■ They used their recordings to explain the changes in the length of the shadows cast over the period of the investigation.

Drawing conclusions
■ They could relate the changes in the shadows cast to the movement of the Sun across the sky and could explain if their predictions were correct or not.

at level 5

Identifying key factors
■ They identified at the planning stage that the stakes must be in a position which will not become overshadowed by any object as the Sun's position in the sky changes. They also explained that recordings must be taken at the same time each week. They were also aware that it would not be possible to take readings on the same day each week because the Sun might not be visible.

Make predictions based upon scientific knowledge
■ The children predicted that the shadows would change in length from day to day because the Earth is rotating around the Sun and so throughout the year the Sun changes its position in the sky.

Select apparatus and use with precision
■ They selected appropriate apparatus for the investigation.

Make observations or measurements
■ They observed that throughout the term the shadows cast from each stake at the same time of day had changed.

Repeat and explain differences they encounter
■ The investigation was undertaken again during a different term. The stakes were placed in exactly the same positions as before. The children made recordings each week at the same time. They observed that there were differences in the shadows due to the Earth's position in relation to the Sun being different from the term in which they undertook the previous investigation.

Recording
■ Careful recordings were taken and recorded on a chart each week. The chart was permanently on display in the classroom. As the recordings were added the children began to see patterns and were able to begin to make predictions about future recordings.

Drawing conclusions
■ The children drew conclusions which were based entirely upon their recordings.

COMPUTER RESOURCES

The following equipment has been found to be the most suitable for use in primary schools. It is recommended that an old BBC computer system be dedicated to computer control so that equipment can be left connected and children can be given opportunities for writing simple procedures to control lights and switches during any spare time they may have. Computer control work will reinforce and extend work undertaken on electricity at Key Stage 2. Computer control equipment and software is available for use on an Archimedes computer.

EQUIPMENT

Deltronics primary 'control it' interface box

This package is available for both BBC and Archimedes computers but although it includes several sensors, there are nowhere near enough and they are not those which are in most common use. Extra sensors can be ordered from G.C. Products. The software *Contact* can be purchased from NCET Publications. Be sure to indicate when ordering whether the BBC or Archimedes version of the software is required.

Deltronics, 91 Heol-y-Parc, Cefneithin, Llanelli, Dyfed SA14 7DL
Tel: (01269) 843728

Primary technology: the place of computer control

This is a very useful pack which includes the software *Contact* required to run the control equipment, in addition to many ideas for activities to be carried out by primary school children.

NCET Publications, Milburn Hill Road, Science Park, Coventry CV4 7JJ
Tel: (01203) 416994

Extra output and input leads (with sensors attached)

Output leads have the larger 3.5 mm jack plugs. The most useful outputs to order are those with lights and buzzers. Lego motors are recommended instead of the cheaper alternatives for control work as they can easily be incorporated into Lego models made by the children. When using Lego motors order extra output leads with Lego motor attachments already fitted.

Input leads have the smaller 2.5 mm jack plugs. The most useful inputs to order in larger quantities are those with LDR (light sensors) and switches attached.

The equipment can be purchased from:
GC Products, The Bungalow, Northbeck, Scredington, Sleaford, Lincolnshire NG34 0AD
Tel: (01529) 306234 or (01529) 305613

Box of Lego Technics 2

Additional Lego motors.
Lego motor speed controllers (gear blocks for use with motor sets 8700 and 880. Lego Part No. 872).

The Lego equipment can be purchased from:

Technology Teaching Systems, Unit 4, Holmewood Fields Business Park, Park Road, Holmewood, Chesterfield S42 5UY
Tel: (01246) 850085

BIBLIOGRAPHY

Teachers may find the following books, listed by publisher, a useful reference source.

The Association for Astronomy
Earth and Space

Classroom
Practice in Primary Schools

DATA (the Design and Technology Association)
16 Wellesbourne House
Walton Road
Wellesbourne
Warwickshire CU35 9JB
Tel: (01789) 470007
Design and Technology – Primary Guidance

Forbes Publications
The Good Health Project

Foulsham Educational
Understanding Primary Science

Health Education Authority's Primary School Project, Nelson
Health for Life 2

Heinemann Educational
My Body Health Authority Project

HMSO Books, London
Science; Key Stages 1, 2 and 3

Lincolnshire County Council, Lincoln
Science at Key Stages 1 and 2

Macdonald 5–13, London
Minibeasts
Ourselves
Trees
Seeds and Seedlings

Metals–Stages 1 and 2
Metals–Background Information
Structures and Forces

Macdonald Educatinal, London
An Early Start to Science
An Early Start to Nature

John Murray Publishers
Primary Science: A Complete Reference Guide

National Curriculum Council, York
Forces – A Guide for Teachers
Electricity and Magnetism
(available from SCAA, Newcombe House, 45 Notting Hill Gate, London W11 3JB)

Northamptonshire Science Resources
Exploring Earth Science

Science Horizons
Our Home
Keeping Our Home Warm
Materials In The Home

Science Now
Plastics A Plenty
Metals and Corrosion
Chemicals On The Farm
Electricity
Inheritance
Biotechnology
The Body In Action

Technology Teaching Systems
Electricity Book 1
Electricity Book 2

The following books, listed by publisher, provide useful resources for children.

Blackie Academic and Professional, Glasgow
Sound

Dorling Kindersley, London
My Science Book of:
Electricity
Magnets
Light
Colour
Sound

Eyewitness Visual Dictionaries:
The Visual Dictionary of Plants
The Visual Dictionary of Animals

Eyewitness Guides:
Fossil
Rock and Mineral
The Earth and How It Works
Fish
Seashore
Pond and River

Mammal
Insect
Butterfly and Moth
Shell
Plant
Bird
Skeleton
Amazing Spiders
Amazing Frogs and Toads

Ginn Science, Aylesbury
Sound
Wood and Paper

HarperCollins, London
Key Stage 1 Toys

Thomas Nelson, Walton-on-Thames
Science – Start Here:
Making it Move
Making Changes

Oxford University Press, Oxford
The Young Scientist Investigates:
Seeds and Seedlings
Flowers
Tress
The Human Body
Air
Water
Rocks and Soil
Everyday Chemicals
Materials
Into Science – Weather

Usborne, London
Planet Earth
Children's Encyclopedia of Prehistoric Life

Wayland, Hove
Water